GOLF TIPS FROM THE STARS

GOLF TIPS

FROM THE

STARS

EDITED BY BILL ELLIOTT
AND MITCHELL PLATTS

ILLUSTRATED BY
PAUL TREVILLION

LIMITED EDITIONS
BOOKTITLES

CONTENTS

This edition published by
Limited Editions 1994

An imprint of Random House (UK) Limited
20 Vauxhall Bridge Road, London SW1V 2SA

Random House New Zealand Ltd
18 Poland Road, Glenfield, Auckland

Random House South Africa (Pty) Ltd
PO Box 337, Bergvlei 2012, South Africa

First published 1993 by Stanley Paul & Co. Ltd

Copyright © Bill Elliott and Mitchell Platts
1993

Illustrations © Paul Trevillion 1993

The right of Bill Elliott and Mitchell Platts to be
identified as authors of this work has been
asserted by them in accordance with the
Copyright, Designs and Patents Act, 1988

Set in Palatino and designed by
Brian Folkard Design

Printed and bound in Italy by
New Interlitho, Milan

A catalogue record for this book is available
from the British Library

ISBN 0 09 178806 4

FOREWORD

Golf is a game to be enjoyed but never mastered. Part of the charm of golf is the fact that no matter how well any of us play one day we cannot be sure how we will perform 24 hours later. This is true of me in the Open Championship and you in your club competition. And there is no short cut to playing to the best of your ability. No matter what level you play at, you must spend time on the practice range and putting green. It takes many hours, sometimes many years, to groove a swing so that it repeats and the moment you think you've got it is when you must work even harder. This is why, more than any other game, golf is a voyage of discovery – and many times each of us must be prepared to crash on to some rocks on the way. Yet still we come back, each of us attracted by the many and varied challenges of the game. Of course the amateur will never have the time to devote to his or her game that we professionals have, but he can improve his game by picking the brains of the world's best players. There is no question that by keeping it simple you can knock shots off your handicap. And keeping it simple and easy to understand is what Bill and Mitchell have set out to do in this book. There are, of course, many instructional books on the game of golf, several of which I am proud to be associated with myself, but what this book seeks is to pass on the tricks of the trade from the likes of Arnold Palmer, Jack Nicklaus, Sandy Lyle, Greg Norman, Nick Faldo, Gary Player and, of course, myself. I have known Bill and Mitchell throughout my career and they have been on the right side of the fairway to talk to all the great players throughout theirs. I hope that the secrets they pass on to you through this book help to lower your handicap and, above all, to enjoy the game more. Some of these tips I agree with, some I do not, but this is not important because what might fail me, might well succeed for you. I am sure, however, that this book, superbly illustrated by Paul Trevillion, will help you to enjoy even more the greatest game in the world. Pay attention to this book and I am sure you will indeed improve your golf.

Best wishes and good luck

Seve Ballesteros

Severiano Ballesteros

INTRODUCTION

Few games can boast as many experts as golf. Even the average player carries with him, or her, an opinion on how this shot, or that recovery, should be played.

It is the same in the professional world. There is not a pro golfer on earth who has not been helped out of a career trough – or temporary hiccup – by a serious rival who has spotted a flaw on either the practice ground or the putting green.

Such information and analysis is freely given. Always. It is as though all golfers are part of the same family – and indeed this is more or less the case. Certainly, playing golf has brought us more pleasure than any other game but it has brought suffering to us as well. This is a universal experience, for no other game can be as perverse.

It is not the pain of a high tackle or a low blow, but it still hurts. Suddenly, the shot you have played comfortably, if not well, all summer seems as alien as a plastic driver. Just when you think your golf has never been better, it tends to get dramatically worse. It was out of this relentless sporting truth that the idea for this book was born.

Between us, we have watched golf being played at the highest level for more than thirty years. Invariably we have been inside the ropes. This has been a privileged position from which to view the blossoming of the game in Europe and beyond and, of course, to witness the emergence of the likes of Ballesteros, Faldo, Lyle, Woosnam and Langer.

Many players have become friends. Some, it has to be admitted, remain polite adversaries. Whatever the relationship, however, each player we asked was willing, eager even, to pass on their knowledge. The result has been this book.

We are, of course, indebted to each player for his or her contribution. It is without doubt a unique compilation. But the following pages are not intended to teach you how to play golf. This is no starter pack. There are enough of those around without us adding to the list.

Rather, this is the collected wisdom of the people who play the game for a living. Each of these professionals has learned the hard way just what the key clues are to this baffling game, of how to escape from brutal situations, how to remain in control when every instinct encourages panic.

Read this book and we believe that you will discover truths you had not realised, perhaps unearth the tips that will transform your game. The overall intention, however, is to help you enjoy your golf and to have more fun on the course. It is, after all, only a game. Isn't it?

Bill Elliott
Mitchell Platts

THE SWING

· SEVE BALLESTEROS ·

Severiano Ballesteros. Height: 6ft. Weight: 12st 9lbs.
Birth date: 9 April 1957. Birthplace: Pedrena, Spain

Seve Ballesteros is acclaimed as the most inspired shotmaker of his generation. The son of a farmer, his uncle, Ramon Sota, was one of Spain's best-ever golfers and his three older brothers are all professionals. One of these brothers, Manuel, started Seve on the road to fame, fortune and a niche in the game's history when he cut down a three iron and gave it to Seve as a little boy. For the next several years he honed his game, hitting first pebbles and then old balls on the beach near his home. A winner all over the world, wherever he has played golf, his finest moment came when he won the Open Championship at St Andrews in 1984, just one of his major titles during a career that has sparkled since the mid-seventies. Ex-Ryder Cup captain and former Open champion himself, Tony Jacklin sums up Ballesteros thus... 'He is not only a great golfer, he is a great man. I am proud to call him a friend.'

The Tip

NAIL THAT RIGHT SIDE

Nothing is more important than getting the right side out of the way on the backswing so allowing a full turn. My key move for a drive off the tee or a long iron from the fairway, is, when everything else is settled, to imagine a nail being hammered through my right buttock. It means I move my buttock no more than two inches back but this is sufficient to encourage me to turn correctly and it also means I turn smoothly. Nothing in the golf swing should be jerky or feel hurried. It is a very simple tip – but then I have found that these are the best.

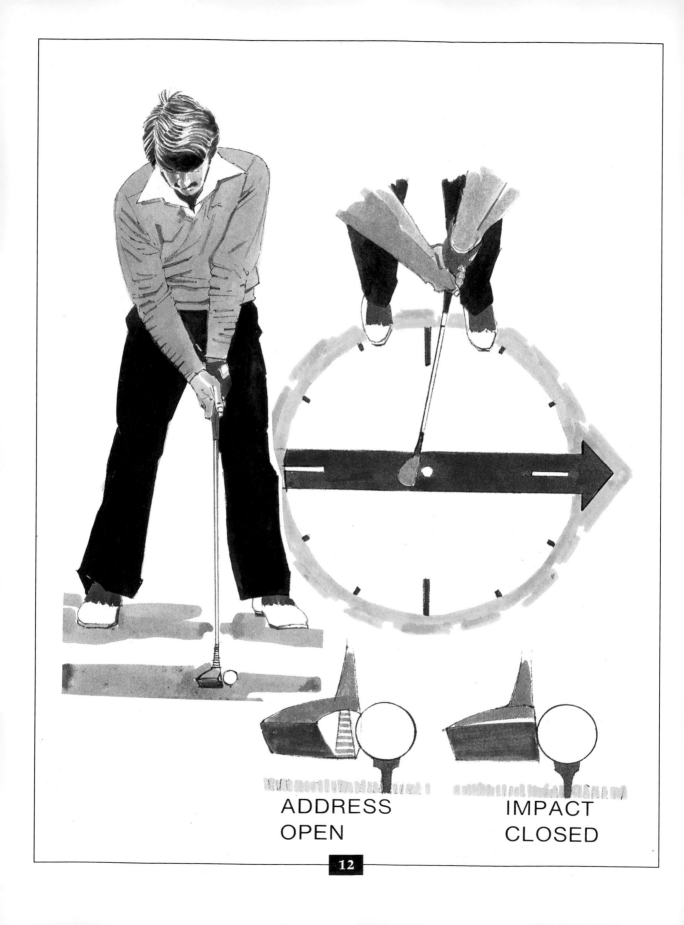

ADDRESS
OPEN

IMPACT
CLOSED

· PETER McEVOY ·

Born in London on 22 March 1953, McEvoy is simply the finest British amateur of his generation. Twice Amateur Champion in 1977 and 1978, McEvoy has played in five Walker Cups to date and won practically every honour and title available to him. Still at the forefront of the amateur game, he runs his own PR company based at Cheltenham and is universally acknowledged as one of the most talented players never to turn professional.

The Tip

OPEN UP FOR SUCCESS

It is very noticeable to me that 99 per cent of golfers cut the ball. If you look at the average amateur setting up to the ball, you'll notice that mostly they toe the club in. In other words they have the clubface facing left. I noticed when I started to play with good players that those who drew the ball from right to left had the clubface open or pointing to the right. So to get the average player who cuts the ball to draw it what I suggest is that they turn the face of the club wide open, which makes them think they are going to hit the ball right of the target, and then I get them to close the face as they hit the ball. If you are standing at six o'clock, aim at three o'clock and then close the face as you hit the ball. This exercise will train your hands to produce the hit with enough hook spin to work the ball from right to left. It is contrary to normal teaching methods, but it was born of noticing that everyone seems to do exactly the reverse to fade the ball! And it works.

· TONY JACKLIN ·

Height: 5ft 9ins. Weight: 12st. Birth date: 7 July 1944.
Birthplace: Scunthorpe, England

Jacklin's golf career had a glittering beginning and a glittering finale with a deep trough in the middle. He achieved fame when he won the 1969 Open Championship at Royal Lytham in 1969 and 11 months later added the US Open title to his collection. Although he won 14 European Tour titles before winding down, a combination of occasional ill luck and poor putting cost him many more chances of victory. Then just as his name was fading, he achieved the greatest fame of all when he skippered the European Ryder Cup side to success against America in 1985 and 1987 before Europe halved the match in 1989 and Jacko stepped aside.

The Tip

THE SHOE-BALL TRICK

The problem for most amateur golfers when they take the club back is that they sway. If you feel this is happening to you, one of the best methods to cure it is to go to the practice range, place a ball under the outside of your right shoe and make your normal swing. The position of the ball will make sure that you cannot sway.

· JACK NICKLAUS ·

Height: 5ft 11 ins. Weight: 13st 3lbs.
Birth date: 21 January 1940. Birthplace: Columbus, Ohio, USA

Jack 'The Golden Bear' Nicklaus started his professional career spectacularly when he won the 1962 United States Open Championship. He added another 17 major titles, including three British Opens, before he began to concentrate on course design. Most people's idea of the greatest golfer of all time, even his few critics acknowledge that Nicklaus is without question the fiercest competitor the game has ever seen. No player has ever taken more care, or concentrated more keenly, than Nicklaus.

The Tip

HEADS YOU DRAW

If you have trouble drawing the ball from right to left then Jack Nicklaus has some advice for you. His first thought is to set his head behind the ball and keep it there. This demands complete concentration. But if you stay behind the ball through impact you will find that you can release the clubhead before the hands get ahead of the ball, which is what you must do if you want to hit a draw.

· ARNOLD PALMER ·

Height: 5ft 10ins. Weight: 13st. Birth date: 10 September 1929.
Birthplace: Latrobe, Pennsylvania, USA

No golfer has ever had the impact of ex-Marine Arnie. He exploded on to the American golf scene in the mid-fifties and his go-for-it style immediately made him stand out from the herd. In his prime, nothing seemed beyond Palmer's aggression and talent. The winner of three US Masters titles, two British Opens and the US Open, he is currently the biggest draw on the US Seniors Tour and still one of the biggest earners in American sport. Apart from his achievements on course, Palmer is also credited with single-handedly turning golf from a minor sport into the mainstream spectacle it is today. Jack Nicklaus, his greatest rival, is credited with saying: 'Every pro should give Arnold a dollar for each dollar earned. That's the debt we all owe him.'

The Tip

SHORT IS GOOD

There are few sights in golf which have stirred the emotions more than Arnold Palmer in full flow. That hitch-up-the-pants-and-give-it-a-rip style is characterised by the breathtaking finish to all his shots. Palmer once said that you can't approach the ball in the same manner as a butcher attacks a leg of lamb. But he has always stressed that you must never slacken off — that hitting the ball is only half the story. It is important to complete the swing and not stop at impact. What Palmer has always preached is that if you don't want to hit a shot flat out with a given club in your hands then the thing to remember is to shorten the backswing, which will automatically shorten the follow-through. In this way you hit a full shot and eliminate the risk of 'missing' the shot through being weak after impact.

· BEN CRENSHAW ·

Height: 5ft 9ins. Weight: 12st. Birth date: 11 January 1952.
Birthplace: Austin, Texas, USA

When 'Gentle Ben' won his only major to date, the US Masters in 1984, the rest of the golf world embraced his achievement. Few players have ever been as popular as the Texan and his Augusta victory ended at last the fear that here was an outrageously gifted player destined never to win a major. One of America's top players since turning professional in 1973, Crenshaw is acknowledged as one of the game's great historians and collectors. Sometimes it has seemed that he is too interested in the game's past to have made the mark he should on its present.

The Tip

THE BARREL TURN

The main thing, apart from the grip and standing comfortably to the ball, is to pivot or turn. It's been likened to turning in a barrel without trying to knock the staves out. You see we must be able to turn in this game and sometimes we use only our arms. We've got to remember it is a full body turn as well. You must turn your shoulders, turn back through it and achieve a nice, high finish. Most people have the misleading image with the barrel theory, that to use it as a turning aid is to think only of the backswing, but you *must* remember to take it back through and to complete that finish still with the thought of turning in the barrel.

· IAN WOOSNAM ·

Height: 5ft 4½ins. Weight: 11st 7lbs. Birth date: 2 March 1958.
Birthplace: Oswestry, Shropshire, England

Living proof that if you are good enough then you are big enough, Woosnam is the epitome of a natural golfer. His swing is simplicity itself, his power awesome, his nerve unquestioned. Yet it was not instant success for the man born in the border town of Oswestry and who proudly claims Welsh citizenship. His early years were studded with disappointment and frustration but he never lost confidence in his ability to make his mark on the history books one day. One of the most prolific winners the European Tour has ever seen, Woosie has underlined his ability by winning all over the world, his US Masters victory in 1991 being the highlight of his career to date.

The Tip

DON'T USE YOUR HEAD

Every player, pro or amateur, should work very hard to ensure that their head stays still through the swing. A lot of amateurs tend to move their heads about even more than they think, or fear, they do. So if you can keep your head still and turn your shoulders around your head then that has to be an advantage. To help do this I suggest that you practise with your feet together. Hit a few shots like that and you will be pleasantly surprised how it will give you increased confidence to keep that head still.

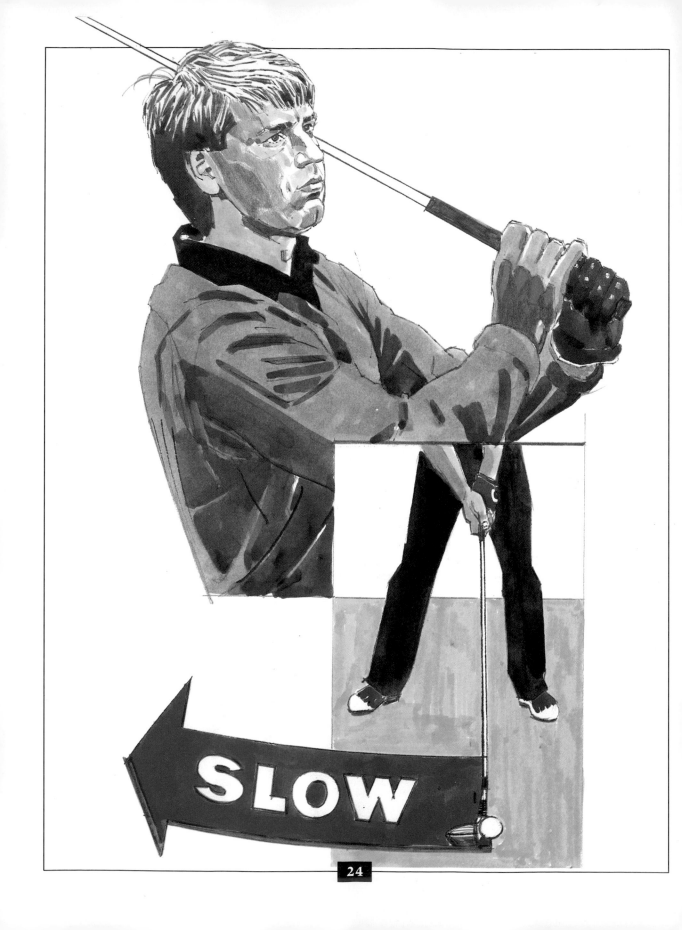

SLOW

· PAUL WAY ·

Height: 5ft 8ins. Weight: 11st. Birth date: 12 February 1963.
Birthplace: Kingsbury, Middlesex, England

Paul Way is an enigma. Good enough to win three European titles, including the 1985 PGA Championship, and to play in the 1983 and 1985 Ryder Cup sides, his game has at times deteriorated to the point of oblivion. Way, however, has never given up, fighting back each time to display again at times the brilliance he showed as a youngster on the European Tour. According to Tony Jacklin he can 'achieve what he wants to out of golf, it's up to him.'

The Tip

SLOW-SLOW-SLOW

I can't stress how important it is to have a slow takeaway. You must have rhythm in the swing and the first step to achieving it is a slow takeaway. The trouble is, of course, finding a way to repeat it time and time again. I believe a good method is to keep on the move. If you watch Nick Faldo, you will see he is always moving. It's hard to get rhythm if you're still. If you're still, you're going to be quick. So it's better to keep shuffling, waggling, moving. You watch most of the great golfers and you will come to notice that nearly every one of them is on the move one way or another until the moment comes to take the club back. Seve Ballesteros is an exception. He stands still for ages. But Seve has great rhythm anyway. Most of us mere mortals need a routine – I certainly do. And let's be honest most amateurs swing the club far too quickly. So if you're quick with the takeaway, you're going to be quick throughout the swing. So watch the stars and find a routine that you think will help your game. Then rehearse it.

· BOB TORRANCE ·

This former Largs, Scotland, club professional now enjoys a reputation as one of the very best teachers on earth. The father of Ryder Cup star Sam, he travels to almost every European Tour event where he has a regular squad of disciples eager to employ his expert eye on the practice ground. He can spot a fault instantly and correct it almost as swiftly.

BOTTOMS UP

If you can get your weight from your left to the right and from your right to the left then you can get away with murder! You can do a lot of things wrong but if you do that correctly then I think you will play good golf. Sometimes I get players to swing from their left toe to their right heel and from their right toe to their left heel. You can do that as an exercise without hitting the ball. The other way is to point the left knee at the ball at the top of the swing and point the right knee to hit it. I think if you're bad in the bottom half of the body, then you're bad everywhere. I think the game begins and ends from the hips down. If you get that part of the game right then you can do five things wrong and still hit the ball well.

· DAN HALLDORSON ·

Height: 5ft 10ins. Weight: 12st. Birth date: 2 April 1952.
Birthplace: Winnipeg, Manitoba, Canada

Golf came naturally enough for Halldorson, who was brought up beside a course. He even built his own driving range in the family backyard as a youngster. The Canadian first qualified for the US Tour in 1974 and enjoyed his greatest success in 1980, when he won the Pensacola Open and then teamed up with Jim Nelford to win the World Cup. In 1986 he joined Dave Barr to bring Canada another World Cup team trophy. He has twice been voted the Canadian Playing Professional of The Year.

The Tip

WALK A TIGHTROPE

Balance! That's the secret of a good golf swing. The moment any of us starts falling over we are heading for trouble. Deep trouble. Work on being properly balanced. Swing your arms to and fro as hard as you can without over-balancing. Think as though you are trying to walk a tightrope and get on the balls of your feet. Discover the right width to have your feet. If it's a full-out shot then widen your stance a bit and always try to hit the ball with your practice swing. Ask the average player to swing without a ball and he does it pretty well. Then ask him to hit the ball and he turns into Quasimodo.

· GARY PLAYER ·

Height: 5ft 7ins. Weight: 11st. Birth date: 1 November 1935.
Birthplace: Johannesburg, South Africa

As long as golf is played, the name of Gary Player will be listed with the all-time greats. Winner of more than 100 professional titles all over the world he also claims to have travelled more than anyone else during his four decades as a pro. He has won nine major titles, three Open Championships, three US Masters, two US PGAs and the US Open. The original health freak, Player says he weighs the same now as he did 35 years ago although, if anything, he is even more competitive no matter what game he is playing. He has also never been known to allow the facts to get in the way of a good story.

The Tip

PULL THAT LEFT HAND

You know, the best tip I can give you, is to take the left hand from the top of the back swing and pull down with it. Don't cast. Don't throw from the top — pull down! The reason? Well, if you pull down with the left hand, you must approach the ball from the inside which will automatically lead to your weight getting across to the left side. That will in turn lead to a good follow-through and the completion of a solid swing.

· COREY PAVIN ·

Height: 5ft 9ins. Weight: 10st. Birth date: 16 November 1959.
Birthplace: Oxnard, California, USA

Pavin blazed a unique trail when he joined the European Tour in the early eighties to sharpen his game. He spent just one year in Europe but won the German Open before returning to America and his US Tour card. He has established a reputation as an aggressive golfer who on his day can 'shoot the lights out'. In 1991 he was the leading money winner on the US Tour and voted the PGA of America's Player of the Year. His success in the 1992 Honda Classic was the tenth on the US Tour.

The Tip

THE OLD ONE-TWO

The one most important thing is to have a very good tempo and rhythm to your swing. I know it's hard when you don't play a lot but it is the one thing I see that changes more often than not with the average player. You can see the tempo changing from swing to swing. I know it is a difficult thing to work on but it can be done. What I like to work on, and sometimes I do it when I'm playing in a tournament, is to take a practice swing and stop that swing at the top. I count myself out by calling one at the top of the swing and then two to start downwards and through it. That really helps my rhythm. I believe it should help all amateurs.

· CHRISTY O'CONNOR Jnr ·

Height: 5ft 11ins. Weight: 12st 10lbs. Birth date: 19 August 1948.
Birthplace: Galway, Ireland

Nephew of the legendary Irish golfer Christy O'Connor Snr, Junior is one of the most popular players in Europe with his prowess as a musician of sorts almost more revered than his ability on the golf course. Steady rather than spectacular, his career highpoint came during the 1989 Ryder Cup at The Belfry when he demoralised America's Fred Couples with a two iron to three feet at the 18th.

HOW TO GET HIP

The one thing which I notice time and time again is that amateurs do not complete the shoulder turn. It is very, very important but it seems few pay any attention to it. The first thing to check is that your left shoulder is under your chin at the start of the down swing. Then comes the important bit because most people only take the club back with their arms; they don't turn their shoulders. The tip to get out of what is a bad habit is to use the right hip to start yourself off on the takeaway. It makes you turn the body by getting the right hip out of the way. But a lot of people just stand there expecting it all to work together; they don't use their legs at all which is so important. They hit everything with their arms. They think they are hitting the ball with all their strength. In fact they are just lashing at it so that they don't hit it as far as they think they are. And, of course, if you hit with the arms then you're hitting from the top — you're not hitting through the ball.

· COLIN MONTGOMERIE ·

Height: 6ft 1in. Weight: 13st 11lbs. Birth date: 23 June 1963.
Birthplace: Glasgow, Scotland

Montgomerie was an amateur of the highest pedigree winning, amongst other titles, the Scottish Amateur and playing in the 1985 and 1987 Walker Cup sides. His progress as a professional since 1987 has been relentless, with victories on Tour and inclusion in the 1991 Ryder Cup side. A natural fader of the ball he appears deceptively cautious but his birdie blitzes on many courses prove otherwise.

The Tip

PEG IT OUT

I'm convinced that it is important to get the first two feet of the takeaway right. You must take the club back low and slow. To achieve this, put a tee peg on the ground two feet behind the ball. Then take the club back, brushing the ground, until you clip the tee peg. You can then start to pick the club up and continue the takeaway. But keep it slow and smooth. Too many amateurs get jerky... and if you get jerky then you won't repeat the swing which is what we are all seeking to achieve.

· SANDY LYLE ·

Height: 6ft. Weight: 13st 5lbs. Birth date: 9 February 1958.
Birthplace: Shrewsbury, England

Although born in England near the Welsh border, Lyle is a passionate Scot who was reared to play golf. The son of a professional, he had a club in his hand from the age of three and has since astounded everyone with his natural power off the tee. Lyle became a national British hero when he ended a 16-year wait by winning the 1985 Open Championship at Royal St George's. Europe's No. 1 golfer three times since 1979, Lyle has won all over the world and is acknowledged as one of the finest 'golfing brains' of his generation. He became in 1988 the first British golfer to win the US Masters and his success in the Volvo Masters in 1992 was his 28th as a professional.

The Tip

REMEMBER THE FEET

I liken the golf swing to that of a dancer: if your feet are in the wrong position then the routine is always going to be awkward. You've got to set up right to the ball or it will be the last waltz for you. The basic principles of the set-up remain the same for everyone – ball towards left heel, balance slightly forward and so on – but YOUR position will be unique so you have to experiment to find out what works best. And remember – stand tall, don't hunch over the ball, which is a common fault among amateurs and throws everything out of control.

· DAVID LEADBETTER ·

The tall Englishman never quite made it as a Tour player but has established a glittering reputation as a teacher. It was to Leadbetter that Nick Faldo turned when he wanted to rebuild his swing and when Faldo became World No. 1, Leadbetter's own prestige soared accordingly. Now based in both Florida and England, Leadbetter has so many devotees to his methods that he has to train special assistants to cope with demand.

The Tip

NAVEL MANOEUVRES

Probably the best thing any amateur can practise is to start the butt, or grip end of the club, back in company with their navel, so that in essence they work together at the same time. When they start swinging the club back, most people just move their arms without using their body. The trick is to get the triangle formed by the hands, arms and shoulders moving together with the navel at the start of the takeaway. This can make such a difference to the quality of your shot. Good luck.

· TONY JACKLIN ·

'Winning the US Open proved that my British Open victory was no fluke. It's always been my contention that the winners of major tournaments are the true champions, although at times some luck may play a part in the victory. Naturally, after I won the British Open, I entertained some suspicious thoughts about luck, but when I won the US Open, this was all dissolved.'

(For biographical details, see p.15.)

The Tip

KEEP SOMETHING BACK

Always play within yourself. The average player hits full-out shots eight times out of ten and this is daft. To maintain tempo you should only hit at 80 to 85 per cent of your potential. I recall the way I hit my final drive at Lytham when I won the Open in 1969. I didn't try to hit the ball, I just swung the club nice and easy, concentrating on rhythm and timing and it worked. If I'd gone at it like the average golfer then the ball could have gone anywhere. Jack Nicklaus told me later it was a great shot. He was right. The fact is that if you swing well within yourself then the *hit* comes naturally.

SLOW AND SLOW

· MIKE HARWOOD ·

Height: 6ft 4ins. Weight: 13st. Birth date: 8 January 1959.
Birthplace: Sydney, Australia

The tall, lanky Australian has a deceptively lazy-looking swing that disguises a man of searing ambition and total self-belief. After joining the European Tour in 1986, he has been one of the leading members of the 'Oz Mafia' that has at times threatened to dominate the golf scene. Harwood has been a winner all over the world; his European successes include the PGA Championship, Volvo Masters and European Open. He divides his life between Melbourne and Surrey's Bagshot.

The Tip

BE PRECISE

Concentrate on taking your club away on the right line. In other words take it back in the precise direction you wish to drive the ball forward. It helps to do this if you first step behind your ball and pick out a spot a few inches behind it that you wish to take the club back over. Then concentrate on pushing the club back as wide as you can to create the right arc before beginning the downswing with your legs. Far too many players I see take the club back outside the line and then compound the error by picking it up too quickly. This inevitably leads to them coming over the top when they begin the downswing and then the ball goes anywhere. There's no need to worry about how far to take the club back along the line because your body will tell you when to stop and begin the ascent. The secret is not to force anything but to have an idea of what you are actually trying to achieve.

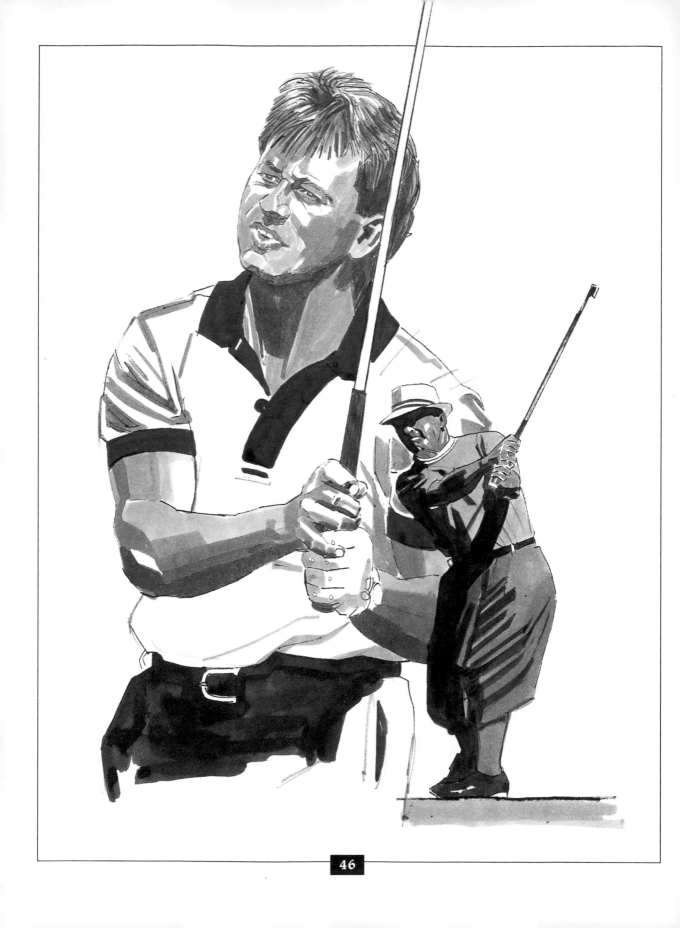

· IAN WOOSNAM ·

'I usually know when I am going to win, or at least be in with a strong chance. It's just a feeling I get but it's very strong and usually I do very well on those weeks. But I don't know how to create this feeling. I wish I did.'

(For biographical details, see p.23.)

(For biographical details, see p.23.)

The Tip

THEY GOT RHYTHM

I always advise amateurs to keep their rhythm and tempo correct. If they don't know what the right tempo is — and most don't — then they should try to do two things...either get hold of some old film of the great Gene Sarazen playing or simply watch Nick Faldo because Nick has the best tempo in the world these days. He never gets too quick or too slow and that is largely the reason why he is so consistent.

· MAX FAULKNER ·

Born at Bexhill in Sussex in 1916, Faulkner was a brilliant if eccentric golfer, his career gloriously crowned by victory in the 1951 Open Championship at Royal Portrush, Northern Ireland, the only time the Open has not been played in either England or Scotland. The first British pro to wear highly colourful clothes, Faulkner was an enthusiastic entertainer who never used a matched set of clubs and who owned over 300 putters.

The Tip

A HARD FACT OF LIFE

The harder you hit the ball then the more the fault is likely to become apparent. For instance I've rarely seen anyone with a two-figure handicap come into the back of the ball from the inside. Mostly they come from slightly outside and with too steep an arc. Hit it harder doing that and a gentle slice will become a vicious one. It is a fact that for the average player to achieve any degree of consistency then the club must be taken back and brought down in the same arc and the results will be better if that arc is on the inside.

· RODGER DAVIS ·

Height: 5ft 10ins. Weight: 12st 2lbs. Birth date: 18 May 1951.
Birthplace: Sydney, Australia

Davis's is a rags to riches to rags and back to riches story. The Aussie stepped off the European Tour in the early eighties and opened a hotel business back home only for financial disaster to strike. Forced back on tour he has played better then ever since his return and become a millionaire once more. Capable of winning anywhere, Davis remains one of those high-class golfers apparently destined never to win a major but his reputation with his peers is of the highest order with more than 20 victories worldwide.

THE LATE HIT SECRET

The biggest problem I would say for most amateurs is that they have difficulty in using their legs. The important thing to know is that it is from the legs that you obtain distance. You can see that just by watching the likes of Ian Woosnam. He transfers the weight so well, with the legs working so quickly, that the hands are delayed to the point where we get what is called a late hit. You will see the professionals take divots because they are driving their legs so hard that they hit down and through the ball. Most amateurs scoop the ball off the top because they don't use their legs. The easiest way to think of using your legs when you're on the practice ground is by kicking the left knee to the target from the top of the backswing. If you achieve that, then you will automatically transfer your weight on to your front foot. To get the best late hit it is necessary to have 90 per cent of your weight on the front foot at impact. You see no matter how hard you drive from the top of the swing, if you drive the left knee into the target then you will get the late hit that I think will improve your overall game.

· PETER COLEMAN ·

This English caddie has been widely recognised as one of the best in the business by colleagues as well as players for a dozen years or more. One of the founder members of the caddies' own professional organisation, Coleman once worked with Seve Ballesteros but has made his name and fortune alongside Bernhard Langer. The slim, serious German and the stocky, bubbly Londoner make an odd couple but theirs is one of the most enduring and successful partnerships ever in golf. In a previous life, Coleman was an assistant pro himself and is still a dangerous, single-handicap opponent.

The Tip

TEMPO EQUALS DISTANCE

I would always say that the one thing amateurs must concentrate on is keeping their tempo throughout the swing. I think the amateurs I see playing alongside Bernhard in Pro-Ams tend to think they hit the ball further than they do. They stand there with 150 yards to go to the green and reckon that they can hit a seven iron to the target. In fact they should be hitting a six iron; possibly a five iron. The trouble is that they know, in the backs of their minds, that the seven iron is not enough. The result? They swing far too fast. Yet if they concentrated on tempo then they would get a range of distance with their clubs which would lead to more consistent hitting. The value between each club is usually around ten to 11 yards. So if you know you hit a five iron 150 yards then use it for a 150 yards shot. Most amateurs tend to believe they can think like a professional, whereas, logically, they should play to their own strengths. And it you don't think that you can hit a ball a long way without hitting it hard then take a look at Woosie. You would never think he is hitting the ball hard. It should be rewarding for any amateur to take a look at a guy his size hitting the ball out of sight without hammering it. It is a guideline to distance. A guideline that tempo will enable you to hit the ball further without hitting it hard.

· DEANE BEMAN ·

Beman became Commissioner of the US Tour in 1974 and has dominated the American professional golf scene ever since. He won the United States Amateur in 1960 and 1963 and became one of the few men to add the British Amateur title. At 29 he turned professional and during his six year pro career he won four tournaments before retiring to 'run the office'.

AIM LEFT TO BE RIGHT

I'd say, and I believe it rings true for *every* player, that the most important thing is aiming left. You've got to aim with your shoulders and your hips left of the target. That will improve everyone. I'm not talking about opening the stance. It is the shoulders which should be left of the target. The reason for this is that it facilitates a better turn and a proper turn. It doesn't allow a tilting of the shoulders but promotes a turning of the shoulders. It also allows you to make a fuller backswing without crossing the line at the top.

· BILLY ANDRADE ·

Height: 5ft 8ins. Weight: 11st 4lbs. Birth date: 25 January 1964.
Birthplace: Fall River, Massachusetts, USA

One of the outstanding amateurs of his generation, Andrade is yet another alumni graduate from the famed Wake Forest University where he studied sociology. Small and slim, he admits he has to rely on a near flawless technique to stay anywhere near the biggest hitters on the US Tour. Clearly his technique is sound, however, for Andrade won the Kemper Open and Buick Classic in back-to-back weeks in 1991.

The Tip

GOLF'S A DRAG

Golf is a difficult game to play at any time, but it is during those moments of tension that it can become impossible. We've all felt our forearms suddenly become tight and lose their feeling as we stand on that final tee, the prize within our reach. It's crucial at these times to make as smooth a takeaway as is possible and I've found over the years that the best way for me to achieve this objective is to concentrate on *slowly* dragging the clubhead back from the ball. It's the same feeling as though you were dragging a heavy object on the end of a rope and what it does is slow the swing down and give you an image to concentrate on at the start of the swing. This sort of movement also prevents you picking up the club too steeply because of tension. After that, if you've practised enough, the rest of your swing will take over automatically. At least, that's the theory.

· TONY JACKLIN ·

'If deep down you don't believe you are a bit better than everyone else then you never will be. Call it self-belief or arrogance, but without it you are a natural runner-up.'

(For biographical details, see p.15.)

(For biographical details, see p.15.)

The Tip

TO START YOU MUST FINISH

Finish the backswing. And finish it properly! I've seen the game played for 40 years and that is the single most common mistake made by anyone, pro or amateur. I reckon 90% of people try to hit the ball too hard. Think rhythm all the time and remember that all the great players complete the backswing all the time. There is almost a pause at the top with these guys. Even quick swingers like Lanny Wadkins or Jose Maria Olazabal do it. They know, I know, and you know that if you try to thrash the ball it won't go anywhere.

· GENE SARAZEN ·

Born in Harrison, New York on 27 February 1902, Sarazen is truly a legend. Winner of the 1932 British Open, two US Opens, three USPGA's (when it was a matchplay event) and the first US Masters in 1935, the dapper, little man still drives the first ball at Augusta each April. His views on the game are still sought eagerly by professionals many decades younger than Gene the Great.

The Tip

GRIP IT CORRECTLY

Amateurs? They've got to get their grips checked. Most of them have it wrong even the ones who think they have it right. The fact is that if you don't hold the club right then you will never be able to hit the ball correctly. I've told every amateur who has ever asked me for assistance to go to a decent pro and have him look over that grip. In most bad grips, one hand dominates the other – so make sure that your hands are working together. Start there or you might as well not start at all.

TROUBLE SHOTS

· SEVE BALLESTEROS ·

'Wherever I am, however I am scoring, you can be sure of one thing...
I am trying my very best on that day. To do otherwise would be
unfair to the sponsors, the fans and it would insult myself.'

(For biographical details, see p.11.)

(For biographical details, see p.11.)

The Tip

WALKING ON WATER

Many times I have seen amateurs hit their ball into the water and immediately
give it up and accept a penalty stroke when, with a bit of care, they could have
played the shot. Two factors must come into play before I will attempt to hit a
ball from the water. First, at least half the ball must be visible above the water;
second, I must be able to achieve a reasonably firm footing when taking my
stance. Then to play the shot I invariably choose a pitching wedge, because this
club not only has loft to lift the ball out of the water as swiftly as possible, but
also because it has a sharp, leading edge which will obviously cut through the
water better than a sand wedge. I position the ball well back in my stance, my
hands significantly ahead, and then make a short, steep backswing before
pulling the club down hard into a spot right behind the ball. Remember to put
on those waterproofs though!

· IAN BAKER-FINCH ·

Height: 6ft 4ins. Weight: 13st 8lbs. Birth date: 24 October 1960.
Birthplace: Nambour, Australia

Baker-Finch graduated to the very top of his profession when he captured the Open Championship at Royal Birkdale in 1991. His final two rounds of 64 and 66 demonstrated his authority from tee to green and his silky putting touch did the rest. His stroke average of 69.92 was the fourth best on the 1991 US PGA Tour. He has won in America, Europe, Japan and ten times 'Down Under', including the Australian Masters.

The Tip

SHOULDERS TO THE WHEEL

Most amateurs should think about using rotation a lot more. I think about using rotation in the swing rather than using the hands. The average player, from a ten to 20 handicap, tends to use his or her hands and arms a lot more than is necessary. The whole body should work as a unit. There should be a lot more rotation in the arms, with them staying as one with the body, which means that from the top of the swing, instead of trying to drive with the legs and hit with the hands, just turn the shoulders. Ian Woosnam is a great exponent of this and, being a lot shorter than I am, his swing looks a lot easier to complete than mine. It is very hard to do it when you are 6ft 4ins tall and long-limbed. But for the tall golfer it is all the more necessary that they use their torso, their upper body, to rotate through the ball. A good tip is to make sure you hit the ball as hard as you can with your right shoulder. That is what I think of. Another thought is to feel the left shoulder going back on the downswing; to feel like it's going away; and to feel that the legs are just a base, that they don't actually do anything, and that the upper body turns back on top of them and through on top of them rather than the legs starting it all. The arms and the hands should lag behind the shoulders rather than lead the shoulders.

· BERNHARD LANGER ·

Height: 5ft 9ins. Weight: 11st. 2lbs. Birth date: 27 August 1957.
Birthplace: Anhausen, Germany

Indisputably the finest golfer ever to emerge from Germany, Langer has been at the forefront of European golf for more than a decade. His worldwide collection of titles is now nudging 40 with the highlight so far his 1985 US Masters victory. It was in the same year that he became the recognised No. 1 player in the world. A devout Christian, this non-smoking, non-drinking sportsman has an enviable reputation as one of the straightest characters in the game as well as being one of the very best iron players the sport has ever seen.

The Tip

MOVE DOWN TO MOVE UP

All of us hit our drives into the rough from time to time. When this happens remember not to be too greedy when deciding which club to take, but at the same time do not be so careful as to cost yourself unnecessary distance. Here is what I mean. Once you have decided that your ball is eminently hittable despite being in long grass, decide what distance you want to hit it. Let us say this distance is 160 yards and that normally you hit a five iron this far. Because of the grass you must now move down *two* clubs to a seven iron. This is because the grass will inevitably wrap itself around the club face and deloft it. So if you use a five iron, chances are the grass will turn it into a three iron and you will top your ball only a few feet forward. Similarly, your seven iron will be turned into something closer to a five iron loft and you will amaze yourself at the distance you will hit the ball. In other words it is okay to be a bit greedy, as long as you *use* the prevailing conditions to help you and try not try to fight them. The more lofted club will go into the grass at a much steeper angle and so pass through much less grass, and the ultimate object is to have the ball get up into the air as soon as possible and so escape the clutches of the grass. It is a technique used by all good players and it is why you may have often been amazed at how we recover from rough situations that have spoiled your Saturday morning round many times in the past. You must also move the ball back in your stance when you play this shot as this enhances the steepness of the approach angle of your club as it hits the grass.

· LEE TREVINO ·

Height: 5ft 7ins. Weight: 13st. Birth date: 1 December 1939.
Birthplace: Dallas, Texas, USA

One of the true immortals of golf, Trevino taught himself to play the game as a poor boy in Texas. A complete natural, he sharpened this talent with a series of private big-money matches against the best of the rest in America before launching himself on to the US Tour. Now predominantly a Seniors Tour player, he is still capable of stunning golf, the sort of play that has won him almost every honour in the game. He started his collection of major titles by winning the US Open in 1968 – his first victory on Tour – and only the US Masters has eluded him. He now accepts he will have to settle for two US Open titles, two Opens and two USPGA victories. In 1990 his first year on the Seniors Tour he won a record seven titles and grossed in excess of $1 million.

The Tip

CROSS YOUR LEGS

I always impress on amateur partners that when it comes to chipping and pitching they should forget about their legs and concentrate on their arms and shoulders. Frequently they find it hard to believe me – or to get their own bodies to react to what their brain is telling them to do. All too often I see an exaggerated leg movement creep into these delicate shots and that usually spells disaster. One great exercise I've devised is to get golfers to stand with their legs crossed so that it is impossible to use their lower body and then have them chip and pitch. It proves to them that what I say is true and it also works as a muscle memory for future shots. If you find yourself having problems with consistently pitching or chipping then cross those legs and hit at least 50 shots just with your arms and shoulders. You'll be amazed at the improvement in your game.

· GREG TURNER ·

Height: 6ft 2ins. Weight: 12st. Birth date: 21 February 1963.
Birthplace: Dunedin, New Zealand

Greg was the third of three sporting brothers to represent New Zealand when he played in the Eisenhower Trophy in the early eighties. Eldest brother Brian played field hockey for the Kiwis, and middle brother Glenn is a past captain and opening batsman for Worcestershire and New Zealand. Greg has been ever-present on the European Tour since 1986 and is one of a select band of players to have won during his rookie season, in his case the Scandinavian Open.

The Tip

TOP HAND GRIP

Not enough players realise that when you are pitching or chipping that the clubface must stay on line throughout the swing. There must be no clubhead flotation, no rotation of those wrists or you will mess up the shot. And the way to ensure this is to grip your club a little harder than usual with your top hand because this helps you hold on to it a little longer. Remember also that the higher you want to hit the ball, the more you open the clubface but wherever the clubface starts is how it must also finish in this shot. I was really struggling with my short game in the late eighties until Rodger Davis passed on this tip and it's the best single golf hint I've ever been given.

· ARNOLD PALMER ·

'Every cloud has a silver lining. Well, this will give the average duffer a bit of heart from here on in.' Arnold Palmer after taking 12 on the final hole of the Los Angeles Open in 1961.

(For biographical details, see p.19.)

(For biographical details, see p.19.)

The Tip

SLICE TO SPIN

One gem of a tip which Arnold Palmer is prepared to share with others is that when faced with a short shot to the green it is best to swing outside the intended line of flight. Practise taking the club back away from you, rather than straight back, because this will put you into a slice swing and automatically produce backspin. Just how far you want to hit the ball is determined by how far you take the club back. But the key thought as you practise this shot must be to take the club away from you.

· GREG NORMAN ·

Height: 6ft 1in. Weight: 13st 3lbs.
Birth date: 10 February 1955. Birthplace: Queensland, Australia

Few golfers of the modern era have hit the golf ball with as much power, or as much gusto, as the tall Australian with the mop of blond hair. Dubbed by many, the unluckiest player ever, after a series of incidents snatched victory away from him in several majors, he did win the Open Championship at Turnberry in 1986. Norman's original ambition was to be a fighter pilot with the Royal Australian Air Force and as a golfer he prefers to fly by the seat of his pants, eschewing the safe route in favour of the most direct. His gung-ho approach has earned him many exciting wins – more than 60 worldwide – and it has also made him one of the highest paid sportsmen in the world, a truly charismatic figure who pulls in huge galleries wherever he performs. In the early 1980s he exited the European Tour in favour of life in the USA and now lives near his boyhood hero Jack Nicklaus in Florida.

The Tip

THREE FINGER TRICK

It might take a little mastering but Greg is convinced that one way to hit those tricky short shots over bunkers, when there is very little green to work with, is to take the pressure off the last three fingers of the left hand just before making contact with the ball. It means you get a flip action, with the right hand going under the left, and the ball will naturally pop up quicker and higher, coming to rest softly on the green. If you complete the shot correctly the bottom of the club should be facing the sky.

· TOM WATSON ·

Height: 5ft 9ins. Weight: 12st. Birth date: 4 September 1949.
Birthplace: Kansas City, USA

Watson's place in golf's Hall of Fame is already assured via his five Open Championship victories plus success in the US Masters and US Open. The USPGA Player of the Year a record six times, his brisk, positive approach to playing golf and his natural sportsmanship have brought him the respect and affection of millions around the world. A psychology graduate from California's Stanford University he is a keenly intelligent and articulate man and his interests spread far outside the narrow area of pro sport. To date Watson has won 32 times in his native America and can boast more than $6 million in US Tour prize-money alone.

The Tip

SPOT THE FLATSPOT

It was definitely the shot of the year – a candidate for the shot of the decade. It was an 18-foot chip from calf-high rough, six feet off the green and downhill all the way. It was struck with a sand wedge and it was in the hole the moment Tom Watson hit it. Watson called it the best shot of his life. It won him the US Open at Pebble Beach, California, in 1982, because Watson holed that shot at the 209 yards 17th hole for a birdie two in the final round and with it condemned Jack Nicklaus to second spot. It was a shot right out of the Watson repertoire because he advocates the theory that it is best to land the ball on the green whenever possible rather than trust the angle of bounce off a severe slope. It is a tip in itself because it teaches one to look for the flat spots on the green; to learn to land the ball there to get the most consistent of rolls with those delicate chip shots.

· CRAIG PARRY ·

Height: 5ft 6ins. Weight: 12st. Birth date: 12 January 1966.
Birthplace: Sunshine, Victoria, Australia

Unassuming Parry is both a highly popular and respected player on the European Tour with the nickname 'Popeye' because of his bulging forearms. His natural talent allied to an aggressive nature on the course has brought several titles already, with everyone predicting an exciting future for this stocky and tough little character. He climbed another Everest when he won the 1992 Australian Masters.

The Tip

HANDS IN FRONT

The secret of most good scores whether you are scratch or 18 handicap is, I am convinced, the art of chipping, of getting up and at least giving yourself an even chance of getting down in two from off the green. And the secret of chipping well is to get one's hands in front of the ball. Far too many amateurs will have their hands vertical to the ball at address or, worse, behind it. It's understandable because it seems logical that to lift the ball into the air you should do this but in fact this scooping action is disastrous. To chip or pitch properly you should have your hands two or three inches in front of the ball so that you hit *down* and therefore lift the ball up. This way, even if you hit it fat or thin, the ball will go forward. And you must go out and practise it. Learn that this simple rule always, always applies in golf and learn by practice and experiment how hard you swing through the ball to get it close from off the green.

· MATS LANNER ·

Height: 6ft. Weight: 12st. Birth date: 3 May 1961.
Birthplace: Gothenburg, Sweden

A regular World Cup and Dunhill Cup player for Sweden, Lanner has been at the forefront of Swedish golf for a decade. Lanner won the 1987 Epson Grand Prix at Chepstow and is consistently among the longest hitters on the European Tour, averaging around 280 yards off the tee.

The Tip

STAND TALL

You will find that if you bend over too much on those little chip shots that you can lose the control you need for that shot and with that your accuracy. It is better to stand tall to the ball because that will enable you to keep your eyes directly over the ball which in turn will stay closer to your feet from where you can exercise greater control. One other tip to eliminate the possibility of fluffing the chip is to imagine that you are swinging a bucket of water without spilling a drop.

· DAVID GILFORD ·

Height: 5ft 10ins. Weight: 11st 3lbs. Birth date: 14 September 1965.
Birthplace: Crewe, England

After playing in the Walker Cup in 1985, Gilford turned professional and has made steady progress through the paid ranks ever since. Quiet and unassuming, he is highly respected as a technician by his rivals and surprised few on the European Tour when he made the 1991 Ryder Cup team after winning the English Open at The Belfry. He was unbeaten at St Andrews as a member of England's 1992 Alfred Dunhill Cup-winning trio.

The Tip

FOLLOW-THROUGH

Most amateurs tend to have a long backswing and then decelerate into the ball when trying to play a shot from out of fluffy grass around the green. They don't have a follow-through. I think the most important thing if you have a long backswing is to stay with that but concentrate on completing a long smooth follow-through. You've got to accelerate through the ball. The key is not to try to play the shot too quickly. Give yourself time, take a practice swing and rehearse what you want to do. You know that the ball is probably going to come out without too much backspin, so you've got to be seeking to hit the ball fairly high and soft. You can't rely on backspin to stop the ball; you want it flopping up into the air and landing softly. It is still going to run further than it would from a good lie so you've got to take that into account.

OPEN

· RUSSELL CLAYDON ·

Height: 6ft 2ins. Weight: 15st. Birth date: 19 November 1965.
Birthplace: Cambridge, England

Claydon's outstanding amateur career was capped by assisting Great Britain and Ireland to victory in the Walker Cup over the USA in 1989. But he also announced his presence when he finished second to Greg Norman in the Australian Masters before turning professional. Claydon, Rookie of the Year on the PGA European Tour in 1990, learned his golf at the admirably named Gog Magog Club in Cambridgeshire.

The Tip

THINK POSITIVE

If you are playing a shot out of ankle-deep rough from around the green then it is best to think of yourself as being in a bunker. So open the blade of your sand wedge as you would in a bunker and aim two or three inches behind the ball. The big tip here is to swing smoothly and to complete the swing. If you quit on the shot then anything can happen to the ball. But if you play the shot in a positive fashion then nine times out of ten you should give yourself a reasonable chance of holing a putt to save your par.

·ROGER CHAPMAN·

Height: 6ft. Weight: 12st. Birth date: 5 January 1959.
Birthplace: Nakuru, Kenya

This former English Amateur champion has one of the most admired swings on the European Tour. No wonder. Although Chapman rarely figures in headlines he is a consistent money winner and has figured in the Top 40 since 1984. A former Walker Cup player he also boasts a low round of 61 during the European Masters in 1985.

The Tip

LOOK UP TO GET DOWN

Don't forget to take a good look at the contours of the green before you pitch to it. The one thing you want to be sure of is that you leave yourself with the easiest putt possible. In essence you always want to be putting uphill. So if the green is sloping away from you, be sure to get the ball to the hole because even if it runs past then at least you will be putting uphill coming back. The hardest thing in the world is to make that four-foot putt which breaks quickly to the right. So don't leave yourself with one to save your par.

BUNKER PLAY

· SEVE BALLESTEROS ·

'I like cowboy and Indian books. During the 1979 Open Championship I read until I forgot my worries and started worrying about the Indians instead.' Ballesteros explaining how he stayed calm before the last round of the Open at Royal Lytham and his first major victory.

(For biographical details, see p.11.)

(For biographical details, see p.11.)

The Tip

STAND BACK IN THE SAND

Over the years I've seen many amateurs have extreme trouble playing a long, greenside bunker shot. Too often they try to pick the ball out cleanly and thin it or else they swing so hard, they dig their clubface into the sand and the ball goes nowhere. The key to this shot is the proper address. Stand a little further from the ball than normal with feet spread wider than your shoulders. This encourages a flattish swing that in turn means you take a shallow cut of sand, sending the ball flying all the way to the pin. It's also helpful on these long sand shots to think of a high follow-through with the hands, as this encourages you to accelerate through the sand under the ball and helps avoid the calamitous 'quit shot'.

· NICK FALDO ·

Height: 6ft 3ins. Weight: 15st. Birth date: July 18 1957.
Birthplace: Welwyn Garden City, Hertfordshire, England

Nick Faldo, arguably, is the best professional golfer ever produced by England. There is, however, no argument that the tall man is the best pupil the game has ever seen. It was, after all, Faldo who detected unsuspected flaws in an apparently graceful and elegant golf swing and decided to reconstruct it. His old swing had carried him to the very forefront of European golf by the mid-eighties but Faldo was unhappy with it and studied for two years under the expert eye of coach David Leadbetter in Florida. What emerged eventually was a player of immense technical ability, and a man filled with confidence. It has proved an irresistible combination ever since with Faldo plundering major titles and establishing himself as the number one player in the world. Faldo's careful approach to the game has been described in some quarters as boring but as he says, 'I thought the point was to try to hit every fairway, then hit every green and then try to hole every putt!'

The Tip

SPOT THE BALL

Nick Faldo recalls that he launched his 'comeback' year – 1987 – by going into the loft and bringing out 30 sand wedges for inspection. He got up and down from the sand ten times out of eleven attempts in the Spanish Open, which he won a few months later. And in the Open Championship at Muirfield he saved par from bunkers three times in four holes from the 7th – including a brilliant 30-yards sand shot to three feet at the 8th – in the last round en route to a memorable triumph. His belief for those long bunker shots is that it is imperative to focus the eyes on the back of the ball. This is to make sure of a clean hit, because if the shot is fluffed it is clear the ball will not reach the target. In other words, all of the ball must be taken and only a little of the sand beyond it.

· TONY JACKLIN ·

'When you are putting well, you can't hear anything off the green but when you're putting badly, you can hear a man jingle two coins in his pocket 100 yards away.'

(For biographical details, see p.15.)

(For biographical details, see p.15.)

The Tip

SOMETHING TO NOTE

Tony Jacklin always advocated that the best way to learn to play the average bunker shot was to imagine the golf ball sitting on a £1 note and to skim the clubhead under it so that it doesn't touch the note. This teaches you to attack the stroke rather than be afraid of it. The days of the £1 note, of course, have long since passed but Tony's tip is still a valid one, even if you have to imagine the ball sitting on a £5 note. That's inflation for you!

· ANDREW SHERBORNE ·

Height: 6ft 3ins. Weight: 12st 10lbs. Birth date: 11 March 1961.
Birthplace: Bristol, England

This tall Englishman is another solid European Tour player who proves that staying power is important. He turned professional in 1984 gaining his card at that year's Tour School but had to return to La Manga in Spain to retrieve his card in 1985 and 1986 after finishing well outside the required money. On each occasion he was successful. He was rewarded for his endeavours when in 1991 he captured the Madrid Open and then won the 1992 Spanish Open.

The Tip

BACK TO THE FUTURE

A long bunker shot terrifies the life out of most amateurs but you've got to think of it as being just another shot. It is still the same club whether you are on the fairway, reckoning on it being a five iron to the green, or if you are the same distance away, with the ball in a bunker. What I would recommend is that you play the ball from a touch further back in the stance and keep the weight more on the left side than with a normal shot. Then concentrate on catching the ball clean rather than hitting the sand. I prefer, too, to look at the back of the ball although some favour looking at the top. But the key is to try not to transfer your weight as much as you would with a shot off the fairway. If you keep the weight more on the left side then you will get a sharper blow on the ball. That way you should hit it clean and not get the dreaded fat one. The golden rule is always to look at the exit path because the first thing is to be sure that you can get the ball up quickly enough with the club you have in your hands so that it does not catch the lip.

· CARL MASON ·

Height: 6ft 1ins. Weight: 12st 7lbs. Birth date: 25 June 1953.
Birthplace: Buxton, Derbyshire, England

Mason's main successes as a golfer have been carved out of the Safari Tour in Africa where he has won three events, the Lusaka, Zambia and Kenya Opens. However, this former British Youths champion has also been second no less than five times in Europe since making his Tour debut back in 1974.

The Tip

BURY THAT SAND WEDGE

It's a minor disaster to go into a bunker but if when you get to the ball you find it buried deep in the sand then straight away most amateurs think they haven't a chance of getting the ball onto the green. It simply isn't true. In most cases you can get that ball out, and fairly close to the cup, if you follow the right routine and if you are positive. The first step is to take an open stance. Then take a full backswing, sand wedge in hand, and swing down hard so that you sink the clubhead straight down into the sand behind the ball. There is no follow through — your aim is just to bury the clubhead as deep as you can in the sand. The more you open the face of the club then the gentler the ball will come out and the less roll it will have on it.

· ANDERS FORSBRAND ·

Height: 6ft 1in. Weight: 11st 8lbs. Birth date: 1 April 1961.
Birthplace: Filipstad, Sweden

Forsbrand was one of the original Swedish golfers to make the European Tour under the tutelage of car giant Saab. He seemed to make his big breakthrough when he won the European Masters in Switzerland in 1987, but a serious swing fault sent him hurtling backwards and he joined the growing band of professionals who turned to David Leadbetter for help. Explained Forsbrand: 'My problem was in the backswing and Leadbetter told me it would take two years finally to get it right. The problem was very similar to Nick Faldo's when he went to David in the mid-eighties.' Forsbrand came good again in 1991 when he won the Volvo Open di Firenze and the Benson & Hedges Mixed Team Trophy with fellow Swede Helen Alfredsson. He also teamed with Mats Lanner and Per-Ulrik Johansson to triumph in the World Cup of Golf by Philip Morris and enjoyed his most successful season to date in 1992, finishing fourth in the European order of merit after winning the Volvo Open di Firenze again and the Cannes Open.

The Tip

FEEL THE SAND

You cannot test the sand in a bunker because that is against the rules but when you step into a bunker and dig your feet in then you can at least feel how much sand there is in the bunker. The less sand there is then maybe the steeper you need to get into the ball so you pick the club up to the outside a little more as this will help you to get the steeper angle you require. If there is more sand than normal then maybe you want to play a shallower shot into it. Then you have to get the weight a little further back in the stance compared with the other one when you get more weight on the left hand side.

· MARK DAVIS ·

Height: 5ft 10ins. Weight: 11st 6lbs. Birth date: 4 July 1964.
Birthplace: Brentwood, England

Davis first joined the European Tour in 1987, three years after winning the English Amateur Championship. A natural sportsman, he has a swing that is admired by other professionals — even the great Seve Ballesteros has been moved to point out Davis's ability. But a combination of illness and injury has affected the Essex player's performance although with his win in a Tour event — the 1991 Austrian Open — Davis is confidently expected to make it back to the top again.

The Tip

THE ALTERNATIVE WEDGE

On occasions it is worth looking at using a putter to get out of a bunker. There is one golden rule: don't try it if the sand is fluffy or if there are rake lines which have caused the sand to be puffy. But if the sand is flat, and there is no lip on the bunker, then it could be the way to get the ball closest to the pin. The key is to make a normal stroke with the ball forward in the stance, so that it is opposite the left heel, which will enable you to strike the centre of the ball with the putter blade on the way up. Concentrate on getting a good roll — and at all times keep the stroke smooth.

PUTTING

· SEVE BALLESTEROS ·

'Sometimes I think the only way the Spanish people will recognise me is if I win the Grand Slam and then drop dead on the 18th green.'

(For biographical details, see p.11.)

(For biographical details, see p.11.)

The Tip

FEEL COMFORTABLE

Many amateurs make the mistake of copying slavishly the putting address position of a top pro. I would never advocate this because it almost always means that you will never feel comfortable and if you don't feel comfortable over a putt, or any other shot, then you are unlikely to strike the ball well. Find out what is best for you, whether that means standing tall over the ball or crouching almost in half like Jack Nicklaus. Even then you will find it advantageous to vary slightly your set-up from day to day or even from hole to hole. I do this all the time. Sometimes I take my 'normal' set-up on the green only to feel that the putter is too long in my hands. So I choke down on it a little, or I stand a little more bent. The key point is to feel comfortable and for us human beings what is comfortable one moment is not comfortable the next. It is like sitting in a chair. After a while we shift position slightly and this is what you should do on the green. Do not always stand open, for example, if on a putt you feel more comfortable setting up squarer to the ball.

· BERNHARD LANGER ·

'I have often been accused of being a slow player. I prefer to think that I am meticulous, that I think carefully before each shot and give myself the best possible chance of striking the ball well. This way I end up playing fewer shots per round and that, in turn, makes me quicker rather than slower.'

(For biographical details, see p.69.)

(For biographical details, see p.69.)

The Tip

YIP-YIP-HOORAY

I do not claim to know more about putting than anyone else, but I do believe that no-one has ever *thought* more about the black art than I have. Given the problems I have had with my putting stroke over the years I have had no choice but to analyse putting if I wanted to continue as a top-line professional. As you probably know, I have ended up using a unique technique whereby I have extended the shaft of my putter by a couple of inches. I grip the shaft only with my left hand and then 'wrap' my right hand over the shaft and around my left forearm. The reason I came up with this idea was to take my right wrist out of the putting equation. It means that my right wrist cannot flex – which is what was happening when I gripped the putter in the conventional way – and so the stroke does not break down. If you suffer from an uncontrolled stroke, call it the yips if you like, then I recommend my method. But whatever style you use to grip the club, I believe the most important thing in putting is to be relaxed mentally and physically. Any tension in your arms or hands and you can expect disaster. This is why you see professionals make all sorts of little movements prior to striking the ball. Jack Nicklaus may be able to stand still for a minute over a putt and remain relaxed but most of the rest of the human race would tighten up severely if they tried to copy him. You must have your own routine on the green and follow it every time. Stay relaxed, stay smooth. This, believe me, is the key to consistent putting.

· EDUARDO ROMERO ·

Height: 6ft 2ins. Weight: 13st 3lbs. Birth date: 12 July 1954.
Birthplace: Cordoba, Argentina

A regular on the European Tour since 1988, the smiling Argentinian has made remarkable progress with four victories in three years, two of them, the French and Spanish Opens in 1991. Romero's easy-going attitude to life is reflected in his style of golf, naturally aggressive with little thought given to possible failure. Many critics feel he is the most naturally gifted player to come out of South America since the great Roberto de Vicenzo.

The Tip

HOVER THAT PUTTER

Little putts are terrible things. Miss one early in your round and the loss of confidence can flow back into the rest of your game like some awful disease. Miss one on the last green and it can cost you the match or the competition and the memory will haunt you until your next round as well. At one time I became very jittery over putts of around two feet and soon it became a real problem for me, costing me many thousands of pounds in prize-money. Then my father Alexander, who is a club pro at Cordoba in Argentina, came up with a solution. He told me not to ground my putter head over these little putts. I tried it and it worked. Now I use this technique all the time. By not grounding the club I keep my backswing smoother and the putter head goes back along the correct line. It is a simple tip but it solves a complex problem.

· SANDY LYLE ·

'It takes a great deal of personal sacrifice to become a consistent contender in the majors. This is why most players are not really contenders. That, and a lack of genuine talent.'

(For biographical details, see p.39.)

(For biographical details, see p.39.)

The Tip

A GRAIN OF TRUTH

I often tell amateurs always to check which way the grain is lying whenever they are putting and it amazes me how many of them do not bother to do this. The fact is that if you are putting with the grain – that is the grass has been cut so that it is lying away from you – the putt will be much faster than if it is facing you. It is such a simple thing but if more golfers paid attention to this detail they would improve their scores by as much as a couple of shots a round. Often you hear a player complain that the speed of the greens varied during his round. It probably didn't alter at all, he just failed to read which way the grain was lying and consequently missed putts he could have made.

· IAN WOOSNAM ·

'When I holed that last putt on the last green at Augusta to win the Masters I knew things would never be the same again.... I knew I'd be better.'

(For biographical details, see p.23.)

(For biographical details, see p.23.)

The Tip

HANDS UP

By holding your hands a little higher when putting, you keep the clubhead on line better. When I start putting poorly I usually end up hunched over the ball, my hands too close to my body and this throws everything out of alignment. This fault creeps gradually into my game as, subconsciously, I end up trying too hard to steer the ball into the hole. Eventually I work it out, stand as tall as I can again and hold those hands higher, almost over the ball itself.

· MARK CALCAVECCHIA ·

Height: 6ft. Weight: 14st. Birth date: 12 June 1960.
Birthplace: Laurel, Nebraska, USA

This outgoing Nebraskan learned to play golf in his bare feet, only switching to regular golf shoes in his teens. A multi-winner on the US circuit, he won the Open Championship at Royal Troon by winning a three man play-off against Australians Greg Norman and Wayne Grady. He says most of his success is down to the fact that his family moved from cold Nebraska to sunny Florida when he was 13 and he discovered it was possible to play golf all year round. He turned professional in 1981 and qualified for his US Tour card six months later shortly after his 21st birthday.

The Tip

FIVE FEET TO HEAVEN

There is no question that amateurs would lower their handicaps and heighten their enjoyment of the game if they consistently holed putts of around five feet. And to do this you must feel ultra-confident from this distance. In other words you must *expect* to hole these putts. For professionals the same can be said of a 15-foot putt. But for amateurs, average amateurs anyway, five feet is frequently the distance they have in order to make par, gross or net. It is why, whatever else they do, that I recommend amateurs to hit at least ten five-foot putts before they go out to play. Get the feel of the distance — and practise from above the hole as well as below it if you possibly can. Becoming proficient from five feet will, I guarantee you, knock shots off your handicap better than anything else.

· BEN CRENSHAW ·

'The reason the Road Hole at St Andrews is the greatest par four in the world is simple — it's a par five...'

(For biographical details, see p.21.)

(For biographical details, see p.21.)

ROLL OUT THE CARPET

In a wonderful career Ben has sunk some marvellous putts, although the one he will never forget is the 60-footer he rolled into the hole at the tenth in the 1984 US Masters at Augusta. It set him on the way to a famous victory. 'The putt had about eight to ten feet of break,' Crenshaw says. 'If I went back a thousand times I wouldn't hole it.' Crenshaw's one thought from that distance is to get the ball close enough to avoid putting pressure on the next putt. But he is a master at making those eight- to ten-foot birdie putts — with a thought process that is as simple as it sounds. If he faces a straight, level putt then Crenshaw 'rolls out the carpet' — he imagines a welcoming red carpet which he sees stretching from the hole to his ball and he putts along the carpet.

· CURTIS STRANGE ·

Height: 5ft 11ins. Weight 12st 2lbs. Birth date: 30 January 1955.
Birthplace: Norfolk, Virginia, USA

Strange has made certain of his place in golf's Hall of Fame with his two US Open victories in 1988 and 1989. These back-to-back wins took his US Tour tally to a stunning 17 victories since he first won the Pensacola Open in 1979. He started playing golf when he was seven and by the time he was eight years old he says he was 'playing every day'. He was helped in this passion by the fact that his father owned White Sands Country Club in Virginia.

The Tip

HOLING OUT STRAIGHT

The Curtis Strange theory — that you will not become a complete golfer and fulfil your true scoring potential until you are a good putter — is as straightforward a statement as is his advice for holing out from inside of three feet. The hot tip from that distance is never to aim outside the edges of the cup, because if you take this approach it means using a slightly firmer stroke, and more often than not you'll pick the ball out of the cup. In other words if you try to be too cute and putt softly allowing for a break then you'll be more likely to end up missing the hole anyway!

· IAN BAKER-FINCH ·

'I'm not a mean person and I never will be. Some people said before I won the Open Championship in 1991 that I wasn't tough enough to win a major. But that wasn't true. I just needed to focus better, not to let outside influences bother me too much. I did learn a lot from playing with Nick Faldo in the final round when he won at St Andrews in 1990. Then all the people inside the ropes and the dust got to me but Nick didn't seem to notice. He was doing what he had to do and he did it well. I might as well just have been a marker out there.'

(For biographical details, see p. 67.)

(For biographical details, see p. 67.)

The Tip

THE 17-INCH RULE

Work on speed on the practice putting green, don't just putt at the holes. The ideal putt is one that, if it missed, the ball would go 17 inches past the hole, which is what all the tests have proved. To putt to a coin, or two tees, is a great putting aid, rather than trying to get the ball in the hole, when you are working on speed or pace of putt. In other words you are thinking of hitting the ball to a certain spot, rather than trying to hole it. If you put a tee 17 inches behind the coin then that gives you a guide. I think just before you go out to play you should be trying to get the ball in the hole to create confidence. But when you practise putting there are a lot of different things you can do and getting a feel for speed is obviously essential.

· TOM WATSON ·

Four times a Ryder Cup player, Watson takes over as captain of the United States team for the 1993 match. He admits: 'There is no question that the pressure created by the Ryder Cup is greater than playing in the British Open. You are testing the human bottle, the human spirit, the human capacity to the utmost.'

(For biographical details, see p.79.)

(For biographical details, see p.79.)

The Tip

TOE IT DOWNHILL

When a player is faced with a tricky, fast, downhill putt I would advise that he deliberately tries to hit the ball with the toe of the putter. By doing this he can still apply a normal strength shot but the ball will come off the face of the club much softer than usual. It gives the player more control and is a much more reliable way of striking a delicate putt than trying to hit the ball softly and maybe quitting altogether.

· PAYNE STEWART ·

Height: 6ft 1in. Weight: 13st. Birth date: 30 January 1957.
Birthplace: Springfield, Missouri, USA

At one time Payne Stewart was in danger of being remembered as an excellent golfer who wore the most colourful clothes on the US Tour. Victory in the 1989 USPGA Championship changed that and by winning the 1991 US Open, Stewart confirmed that he has become a great golfer. One of the few international golfers on the US Tour – he honed his golf in Asia – he was never out of America's top 20 players from 1984 through 1991.

The Tip

LOOKING AHEAD

Most amateur golfers have a tendency to lift their head when putting and in doing so they decelerate the putter. It is a fault which can creep into the games of professionals as well. When I won the US Open in 1991 I tried a little trick and it worked. I started to look two inches ahead of the ball and not at it when I was standing over the putt. That way I hit through the ball and I put an altogether better roll on it. The improvement in my putting was dramatic. If you try it then I'm convinced it will stop you quitting on putts even when you're on fast and treacherous greens.

· GREG NORMAN ·

'Just as I was starting my downswing, a worm popped up right behind my ball and I tried my best to miss it. That's why I hit the shot I did.' A straight-faced Norman explaining to the world's press why he topped one drive less than 20 yards during a European Open at Sunningdale.

(For biographical details, see p.77.)

The Tip

TOOTHPASTE PUTTING

A common feature with a lot of amateurs is that they tighten up when faced with a long putt. My advice is that they should, in fact, do exactly the opposite. The longer the putt, the looser I hold the putter. It is as though I am gently squeezing a new tube of toothpaste. No more than that. This method means that I have more 'feel' and that is vital if you hope to roll the ball up close, or even hole it. If you grip too tightly then there can be a sort of muscle spasm reaction that can result in you rapping the ball way past the hole or even leaving it terribly short of the target. And, of course everyone should always remember that if you are in contention for a title — be it the Monthly Medal or The Open itself — we all tend to tighten up even more so than normal. That is when you must take extra care to loosen those hands and arms on the greens.

NEW ZEALANDER
BOB CHARLES
PROVES LEFT
HANDED PUTTERS
ARE A MATCH FOR
THE BEST

· BLAINE McCALLISTER ·

Height: 5ft 9ins. Weight: 12st 7lbs. Birth date: 17 October 1958.
Birthplace: Ft. Stockton, Texas, USA

Blaine's win in the 1991 Texas Open was his fourth USPGA success in four years — he also won the Vines Classic in Australia — and maintained his dramatic improvement in recent times. A long driver, his iron play is much improved as is his putting — he plays right-handed but putts left-handed.

The Tip

PUTT LEFT-HANDED

If you are naturally left-handed but you play golf right-handed, which is the case for many lefties, then I still believe it is sensible to putt left-handed. I'm a natural 'lefty' and I just find it feels more comfortable to putt left-handed. I also seemed to see too much break when I putted right-handed. You see I do everything left-handed except play golf. In fact, Charlie Epps, the head professional at the Houston Country Club, suggested to me that I should try putting left-handed. I seemed to get more 'feel' and once I got into it then the putts started to drop.

· SANDY LYLE ·

'I like teaching people how to play the game properly. It's very rewarding to see instant improvement. I just wish I could teach myself sometimes but that's harder.'

(For biographical details, see p.39.)

(For biographical details, see p.39.)

The Tip

LOGO WAY TO GO

Next time that you watch a leading pro golfer carefully replacing his ball on the green prior to putting as though he were setting the last diamond into a particularly intricate design, copy him. It may look like a complete waste of time but what he is doing is working out the line and then placing the ball in such a way as the manufacturer's logo points exactly in that direction – just like an arrow pointing out the route to success. It is a simple aid to good putting, a perfectly legitimate one, and one that every amateur golfer should make full use of. Of course, the hard bit is working out the correct line but I can't help you with that...

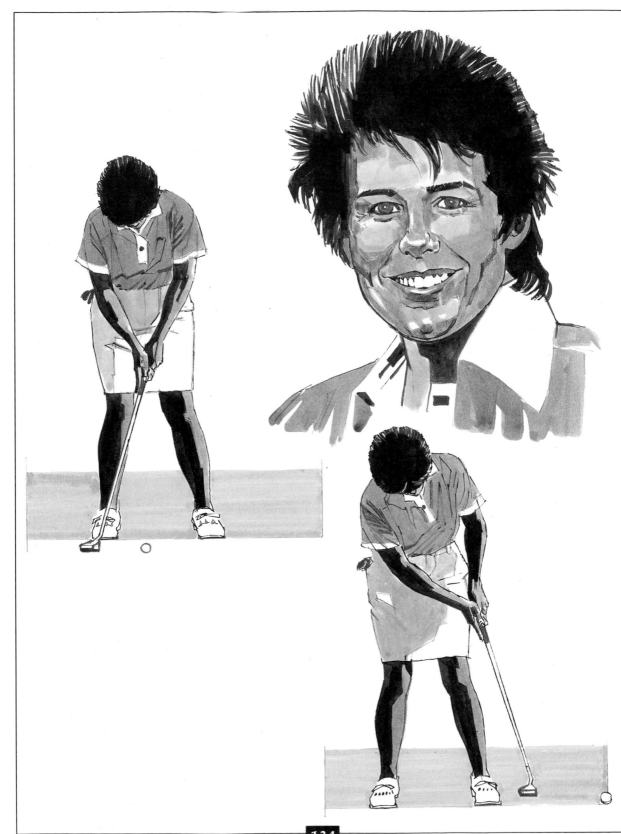

· NANCY LOPEZ ·

Height: 5ft 5ins. Birth date: 1 June 1957.
Birthplace: Roswell, New Mexico, USA

Nancy with the laughing face, they christened her, and they were right because, win or lose, her smile brought life to the women's Tour. In fact she has more than 40 LPGA victories to her name, has set numerous records and earned more than $3 million. The mother of three daughters, she remains one of the most attractive personalities in the game.

The Tip.

SHORT IS BETTER

Where I always give tips is on short putts. This is a vital department of the game. A lot of people when they stand over a short putt tend to get nervous. They start to shake and miss the putt. It's easily done. Let's face it, when given a putt of five feet or less we, as professionals, are meant to hole them and you, as amateurs, expect to hole them. I think the reason why so many putts of that length are missed stems from one thing: we all have a tendency to take the putter back too far then decelerate at impact. What you need to remember for short putts is to take the putter back only a short distance, probably three to four inches, and then accelerate towards the hole, keeping the putter blade going square to your target. I assure you that really helps when it comes to making those putts of five feet and less. You've got to concentrate on keeping the backstroke short and on accelerating through to the hole. Go to the practice putting green and try. I suspect you'll be surprised by how many more of those short putts you make. And if you're confident about holing out then it's surprising how much easier it can make the rest of the game.

INSIDE
INFORMATION

FOR A GOOD
DRIVE HIT A
WEDGE

138

· SEVE BALLESTEROS ·

'The only time I talk on a golf course is to my caddie – and only then to complain about something he has, or hasn't, done.'

(For biographical details, see p.11.)

(For biographical details, see p.11.)

The Tip

DRIVE WITH CARE

Finding the time to warm up your game on the practice ground before a round is always good advice. However, allow me to also advise you *not* to finish off your warm-up session by trying to thunder a succession of full-blooded drives before heading off to the first tee. Most players do this because they reckon the first shot they are going to hit is the drive. In fact, as I once discovered to my cost, ending a warm-up session in this way leads to the wrong tempo and can spoil a round before it has begun. Instead, I strongly advocate hitting just a few drives on the practice tee and always finishing off with wedge shots, because this club will slow down that tempo and stop you getting too 'rushed' before your round has even begun. Where did I discover this truth? During the last round of the Open Championship at Royal Birkdale in 1976. I've never forgotten it....

· WAYNE LEVI ·

Height: 5ft 9ins. Weight: 11½st. Birth date: 22 February 1953.
Birthplace: Little Falls, New York, USA

Levi won his first US title in 1978 and has been a consistent winner ever since. Even he was astounded, however, when he won four titles on the US Tour in 1990. Not surprisingly, he then won the PGA Tour Player of the Year award for his efforts. Levi's other claim to fame is that he was the first golfer to win a Tour title using a coloured ball when he won the 1982 Hawaiian Open using Wilson's Orange Optic ball.

The Tip

TARGET GOLF

I think the average golfer worries too much about the mechanical aspects of the game. I think he would be better advised to concentrate on a few basic principles. You can forget it, for instance, if your alignment is wrong. If your alignment is wrong then all the swing thoughts, all the instruction in the world, are not going to help you. So you must first let someone look at your alignment, teach you about alignment, so that you are lined up in the proper direction to hit the shot. Once you are able to do that consistently then you can build on the rest of your game. You will see more professionals practising alignment on the range more than anything else whenever you go to a big tournament. They will get a fellow professional to stand behind them and ask: 'How am I lined up? Where am I lined up? How are my hips?' I admit it is difficult to get it right. I admit it is easier for us because on the range there is always another professional to turn to for that advice. But I think one thing that you can do to help yourself is to go to the range as often as possible to hit shots at specific targets. Don't just stand there and hit the ball into the distance. You'll grow bad habits if you do that. Get out there and first lay a club down. Get your feet and your hips right. But most importantly get your shoulders right. Whatever direction your shoulders are pointing in is where the plane of the club is going to start and go. You can use your shoulders to shape the shot. If you're going to hit the ball from right to left then you've got to have your shoulders closed; if it's a left to right shot then they've got to be open a little bit.

·JACK NICKLAUS·

'While some Championships are won, most of them are lost. What I've really done is failed a little less than other people who have had the chance to win. The expectation to win has been there my entire career. If I compete, I should win. I feel that way myself. The pressure has always come with the territory.'

(For biographical details, see p.17.)

The Tip

TEE HIGH

The instinctive thought to tee the ball lower when hitting into a strong wind is one with which Jack cannot agree. His theory is that if you do tee the ball lower the likelihood is that you will hit down on it. This will create the backspin which causes the ball to climb higher and higher as it fights against the wind. So Nicklaus advocates that you tee the ball in your normal way and simply concentrate on getting a 100 per cent strike.

· LEE TREVINO ·

'I still swing the way I used to, but these days when I look up, the ball is going in a different direction.'

(For biographical details, see p.71.)

(For biographical details, see p.71.)

The Tip

WET AND CLEAN

Lee grew up living under a hot sun and he won his two Open Championships in the height of the summer. But he found a way to play better golf in wet weather. How often have you hit a shot in wet weather and seen the ball go no distance at all. Too often! Well, take a tip from Trevino and take one club more than you think you need to reach the green. You can move your hands down the shaft a little, which he contends will allow you to get a cleaner strike and reduce the likelihood of you digging deep into mud behind the ball. If you move your hands down the shaft it is clear that you will not get the full distance you hit with that club, but taking one club more will compensate for any loss of yardage. The key is to get that clean strike.

· GREG NORMAN ·

'People still tell me I was stupid to take a driver and knock my ball into that bunker. Well, even I didn't think I could reach it, even I didn't realise how pumped up I was.' Norman explaining his decision to hit a driver off the 18th tee at Royal Troon in 1989, the shot that almost certainly cost him the Open Champioship play-off to Mark Calcavecchia.

(For biographical details, see p.77.)

The Tip

THROW IT TO SUCCEED

Watch a player like Greg as he prepares to play a particularly delicate pitch shot and you will often see him seemingly practising the shot without a club in his hand. In fact what Greg is doing is tossing an imaginary ball to help determine the best method of playing the shot. Norman, like all professionals, is clued-up on the importance of hand-eye coordination — and he often goes through a little routine to keep his hand-eye coordination in tip-top shape. Greg's tip is to cup a golf ball in the right hand, without using the fingers, and then to toss it at target points on the practice putting green. The idea is to vary the height so that you get the feel of stopping the ball close to the hole with a high lob or the pace of a low chip which rolls to the hole. It will help you to visualise a chip better when it comes to having a club in your hand on the course.

· GARY PLAYER ·

'If I wasn't a golf professional then I would either be a rancher or I'd study medicine and muscle development and work on helping young people all over the world improve themselves. I don't know if you'd call it a crusade but I think there's a lot that can be done to encourage people to take care of themselves. To look after your body is the best investment you can make in life.'

(For biographical details, see p.31.)

The Tip

THE DIVOT PIVOT

You've hit a great drive, you walk up the fairway, reach the ball and there it is sitting in a divot hole. You scream 'Why is life so unfair?' Then in your anger you take a club from the bag and swish at the ball – without first thinking how best to play the shot. The first thought should be not to feel sorry for yourself. Then forget all about pulling that wood from the bag. Take a lofted club, position the ball back in your stance – if it is a deep hole then go farther back – and after taking the club up steeply hit sharply down on the ball with the left hand, pulling all the way through to ensure that hands are ahead of the clubhead at impact.

· BERNARD GALLACHER ·

Height: 5ft 8ins. Weight: 12st. Birth date: 2 September 1949.
Birthplace: Bathgate, Scotland

Gallacher was one of the European Tour's original whizzkids beginning his glittering career with victory in the PGA Championship in 1969. In total he has won 14 Tour titles. As an amateur he won the Scottish Open Amateur Championship in 1967. Amongst other highlights, Gallacher has played in eight Ryder Cups and is the current European captain. He is the resident professional at England's famed Wentworth Club in Surrey.

The Tip

FLYING INTO TROUBLE

Sometimes you will see a professional hit a shot, then stare in total disbelief at how far the ball has gone. The odds are that he had got what is called in the trade a 'flier'. You get a flier because you don't get a clean contact between the clubface and the ball when water or grass, for instance, comes between the two. The result is the ball goes through the air with less spin. If you believe that you are likely to get a flier then it is best to take one club less and hit it harder. You see if you hit it easier then you will still get the flier but the ball is quite likely to go even further. So club down and hit harder. In certain circumstances you can hit a seven iron the same distance as a three iron if you get a flier and it can happen from the centre of the fairway as well as out of the rough. So you've got to learn to beware of it happening because otherwise you could hit what you believe to be the perfect shot and watch the ball sail over the green.

· JACK NICKLAUS ·

'I think anybody, any businessman, any athlete who's successful has to be egocentric. I don't think there is a question about that. If you are going to try to be good at something, you can't let somebody else do it for you.'

(For biographical details, see p.17.)

(For biographical details, see p.17.)

The Tip

LOOK RIGHT, LOOK LEFT

A golden rule to remember as far as Jack is concerned is to consider your strategy before you tee the ball up. Too many amateurs rush to get on with it instead of first deciding where to hit the drive. The Nicklaus rule is to hit away from the trouble – if a water hazard lies to the right of the hole, he will tee-up on the right side of the tee and hit for the left half of the fairway. Some tees, especially temporary ones in the winter, are less than flat so it is always important to seek out a level area on which to stand. And don't forget that you can go back two club lengths from the markers.

· BETSY KING ·

Height: 5ft 6ins. Birth date: 13 August 1955.
Birthplace: Reading, Pennsylvania, USA

Betsy shattered the record books in 1989 when, with six wins including the US Women's Open, she earned $654,132 and posted 33 rounds in the sixties. She won 25 LPGA events in her first eight years as a professional – graduating from the supporting ranks to superstar with a self-control that matches her mechanically smooth swing.

The Tip

PLAY THE ODDS

You must play within yourself. You do see a lot of amateurs who attempt to hit shots which they really can't play. You've got to try to play the percentages. If you have a situation where you're hitting it over water with a three wood or you could lay up with another club then have a wedge to the green, then I think more times than not you've got to swallow your pride. You've got to remember that professionals have to do that on occasions so why not amateurs. My feeling as far as gambling is concerned is that if I can get the shot on the green then I'll take the chance. But if it's just to get it closer to where I can get a shorter shot in but if I miss it then it's a penalty situation, then I would probably lay it up. Then when you lay up it is important to leave yourself a full shot into the green. In other words if I can't get it onto the green I don't try to knock it to, say, 30 yards from the green but I try to leave myself a shot of 70 to 80 yards so that I have a full sand wedge. So you've also got to know what distance you hit a full sand wedge or wedge so that you can attempt to calculate the best place to be when going in with that par-saving shot.

· TONY JOHNSTONE ·

Height: 5ft 8½ins. Weight: 10st 3lbs. Birth date: 2 May 1956.
Birthplace: Bulawayo, Rhodesia

Few players have ever approached the game as meticulously as Johnstone. He was the first player in Europe to use a yardage wheel before tournaments and then became the first to plot and graph each green. 'It's such as tough game and I have such trouble reading greens that I want to give myself every chance of success,' he explained as the other professionals giggled. And Johnstone has had the last laugh, winning four titles including the 1992 PGA Championship in Europe and a host in his native Africa since the mid-eighties.

The Tip

FIFTEEN WAYS TO IMPROVE

The average weekend golfer could knock two or three shots off his handicap if he just hit 15 balls before each round. I do a lot of company days and most guys come bolting from the office, or wherever, straight onto the course, panic-stricken, having driven at 150 mph up the motorway, and they think they can stand there and swing smooth and slow! It can't be done. You need to hit those practice balls to get the rhythm in your swing, to get tempo. Look — the average weekend golfer is only playing for fun. I don't honestly think he wants to know about the plane of the swing and all that. But what he does need to do to lower his handicap is to get his own swing grooved into rhythm. I've seen guys rush so fast to get onto the tee that they've even got their spikes on the wrong feet! And I've lost count of the number of amateurs who have hit their first shot so ridiculously quickly that it sends the ball steaming out of bounds. You start with a nine and the day is a nightmare before you've even reached the second tee. If I was to go out tomorrow with a cold start, I know it would take me nine holes to get my rhythm. And I play the game every day of my life. Most amateurs play once a week. It stands to reason they need to warm-up. What do they want to do? Pull three muscles in the back, one in the thigh, or above the hip! Then they wonder why they can't play to their handicap! So give yourself a chance. Make the time to go to the practice area at the club, hit a few balls, get the body relaxed and the mind rid of all those office-thoughts and lower your handicap. I guarantee it will work.

· VICENTE FERNANDEZ ·

Height: 5ft 7ins. Weight: 11st. Birth date: 4 May 1946.
Birthplace: Corrientes, Argentina

Vicente's win in the 1990 Tenerife Open was his fourth on the PGA European Tour and his first since his superb success in the PGA Championship at St Andrews in 1979. He has won more than ten times in South America including the Argentine Open five times. His consistently straight hitting has helped him throughout his career and he is also a wonderful putter, a fact he demonstrably proved when he holed a 90-foot putt on the Belfry's 18th green to win the 1992 English Open, surely the longest putt ever to win a tournament.

The Tip

A TIRED OLD PRO?

If you see a professional yawning then it might not be because he is caught up once again in a five-hour round which much to our disgust have become commonplace in the modern day game. It seems it helps to yawn when you are under pressure. The thinking behind that is that it creates extra oxygen and relieves tension. Try it yourself. If you yawn then you will immediately feel yourself pushing air into your lungs. And it stops you from breathing quickly because of the tension so reducing the possibility of you swinging faster towards disaster.

· DAVID J RUSSELL ·

Height: 6ft 1in. Weight: 15st 8lbs. Birth date: 2 May 1954.
Birthplace: Birmingham, England

A regular European Tour player since 1974, Russell won the now defunct Car Care International in 1985 and then quietly shuffled out of the limelight. Despite being a foot soldier on Tour he has never lost his enthusiasm for the game or his capacity to analyse and talk about golf for hours on end. In spite of, or maybe because of, his size in relation to Ian Woosnam, he is one of the Welshman's closest friends.

The Tip

A GRIPPING STORY

You often hear professionals talking about extra layers of tape underneath the grips of their clubs. I actually play with very little tape because I've got small fingers. But Nick Faldo has played with 12 layers under his grips. You can tell from the callouses on your hands. If you are suffering from blisters, around your fingers or on your hands, then I would suggest your grip size is wrong and that you need to get it checked out by a professional. If you've got long fingers then you are going to need a lot of layers of tape. They also say that the more layers of tape you've got, the less chance you've got of hooking the ball. So if the grips are the right size you should be halfway to hitting a straight shot!

· CHRIS PATTON ·

Height: 6ft 1in. Weight: 14st 11lbs. Birth date: 2 November 1967.
Birthplace: Puontain Inn, South Carolina, USA

Patton won the US Amateur title in 1989 before taking the plunge into the professional pool. He captured the Australian Masters at Kingston Heath to earn his first big prize but he has struggled at the US Tour qualifying schools. All of which is a mystery because he played in the Masters as an amateur in 1990 – and matched winner Nick Faldo's 71 on the opening day.

The Tip

THINK FIRST

I don't believe too many amateurs actually visualise good shots. And I think it is very important to do that if you want to play good golf. If you can get the bad shots out of your head and only picture the good ones then you will be taking a positive step towards making the game a lot easier. How do you learn to do it? It's just time and patience, really. And it is something you really must be conscious of. By that I mean that when you stand over the ball you must know in your mind what you are going to do. You must know what shot you want to hit, you must determine the best way into the flag. You must visualise it. In professional terms it is the difference between being a good professional and being a world class one. So you should learn from that how important it is for you to know what you want to do. It could make the difference between you playing off 15 and off ten.

· RONAN RAFFERTY ·

Height: 5ft 11ins. Weight: 13st 7lbs. Birth date: 13 January 1964.
Birthplace: Newry, Northern Ireland

Rafferty has been marked out as a natural success story almost from the first day he picked up a club. British Boys champion and English Amateur champion before he turned professional in 1981, Rafferty, number one in the Volvo Order of Merit in 1989 with three tournament victories, is surely destined to become one of the world's dominant players in the nineties.

The Tip

THE RIGHT SORT OF CLUB

One of the things I always find when I'm doing company days is the depressing amount of poor, or poorly kept, equipment that people play with. Frequently I discover faults such as clubs that are too light, too heavy, too long or too short. Grips are too thin or too thick for the individual concerned while the grooves can be worn out, or just clogged up with dirt. I can't stress too much how important good, appropriate and well-cared-for equipment is when it comes to playing as well as any of us can. Professionals like myself never stop fiddling round with our clubs and, believe me, we don't do it just to fill in some time. First, you must decide the club that is right for you – and the choice is varied. I suggest you check at any professional's shop – remember, you don't have to be a member – and most will allow you to try out a set before buying as well as advising you. If the pro will not let you try a set, then go somewhere else. It is all a question of 'feel', the wonderful world of 'feel', and you will be amazed how much more feel you get from Set A as opposed to Set B. When you have the clubs for *you* then look after them. I check my lofts and lies every six weeks and change the grips every month. I don't expect you to do the same but you can clean your grips, as I do, by using really hot water, soap and a scrubbing brush and leaving them to dry overnight. It really helps. In fact, I think this is a tip in itself. So don't play a round, throw the clubs in the boot of the car, and get them out a week later for the next round. Remember, look after your equipment and it will help you look after your game.

· CHIP BECK ·

Height: 5ft 10ins. Weight: 12st. Birth date: 12 September 1956.
Birthplace: Fayetteville, North Carolina, USA

Beck, born and raised in North Carolina, became the first golfer ever to be voted Athlete of the Year at the University of Georgia. A stunning amateur record has been swiftly followed by success on the US Tour with more than $4 million in prize-money in 12 years. An outstanding all-round player with several Tour victories to date, he is also an articulate sportsman. This was underlined when, after losing heavily to Seve Ballesteros during a World Match Play at Wentworth, he said he had just 'entered the crucible of humiliation'.

The Tip

ACCEPT DISASTER

I would say that what anyone has to do to improve their game is to enjoy their game. You've got to enjoy, for instance, missing shots before you become good. You see it takes years before you can hit really good golf shots. You've got to digest all the disappointments. You're not going to become a scratch player overnight. You've got to accept that. And to accept it, you've got to keep on enjoying the game. It is always true that what a man thinks he is, is what he is. So you've got to work in the direction that you hope to be. That is just a fact of life. It is just about the best thing that I ever learned.

· JOHN BLAND ·

Height: 5ft 9ins. Weight: 11st 7lbs. Birth date: 22 September 1945.
Birthplace: Johannesburg, South Africa

Bland is one of that élite band of golfers who can be filed under the heading: 'The Professionals' Professional'. Although he has won only twice in Europe, he has captured more than 20 titles on his native South African circuit, including three in 1991 when he finished number one.

The Tip

THE SHIRT-GLOVE

It is obviously very important to keep your equipment dry. We are very lucky because on the Tour we have caddies to do that job for us although, like everyone else, I've carried my own clubs. You must take a spare towel with you out onto the course and dry the clubs off straight after you've hit with them so that you don't put a wet club back into the bag because it will rub up against the others. If you wear a glove and it turns out to be a bad weather day then you've got to protect that glove. The best way I find is to take the glove off immediately you've hit the shot, and lift up your shirt and place it against your stomach. There it can rest against the heat of your body while you walk to your next shot and it will help to keep it dry.

· JOSE RIVERO ·

Height: 5ft 10ins. Weight: 11st 9lbs. Birth date: 20 September 1955.
Birthplace: Madrid, Spain

Rivero is acknowledged as one of the finest strikers of the ball. His cool approach to the game assures him of a top finish almost every time he plays while several European Tour victories prove that his nerve is sound when a winning opportunity arises. He played for the 1985 and '87 Ryder Cup teams when Tony Jacklin described him as an 'essential member of the side'. Rivero hit winning form again in the 1992 Catalan Open in Spain.

The Tip

REPEAT AFTER ME...

Amateurs mostly play just 18 holes a week at the weekend. For them it is a hobby and they should try to relax and enjoy it. Too many try to play like professionals and they cannot. This is our living – it's just a game to you. By trying to emulate their heroes, be it Seve Ballesteros or Jack Nicklaus, they only frustrate themselves and spoil what should be a nice afternoon away from everyday stress. Well, the biggest improvement I can suggest for them is that they do learn from the professionals – but in the right way. For a start they can learn how to concentrate properly. Too many do try to concentrate but they try to do it for every second of a four hour round and that is just impossible. Even Seve, who has phenomenal powers of concentration, could not do it. So learn to concentrate like a pro. We only do it when we are in the process of hitting the ball. Try to construct a physical routine that you repeat each time you approach a shot: make the same number of waggles with your club; look up the same number of times and so on. Good golf frequently occurs because you repeat your swing and by repeating the same physical approach you help to encourage your brain to repeat the movements necessary to repeat the swing itself. Start really concentrating about 25 seconds before you hit the ball and then relax between shots. I talk to my caddy to relax myself but you can enjoy the scenery, chat to partners – anything. The important thing is to clear your mind, and release any tension, before you begin to go through the process all over again.

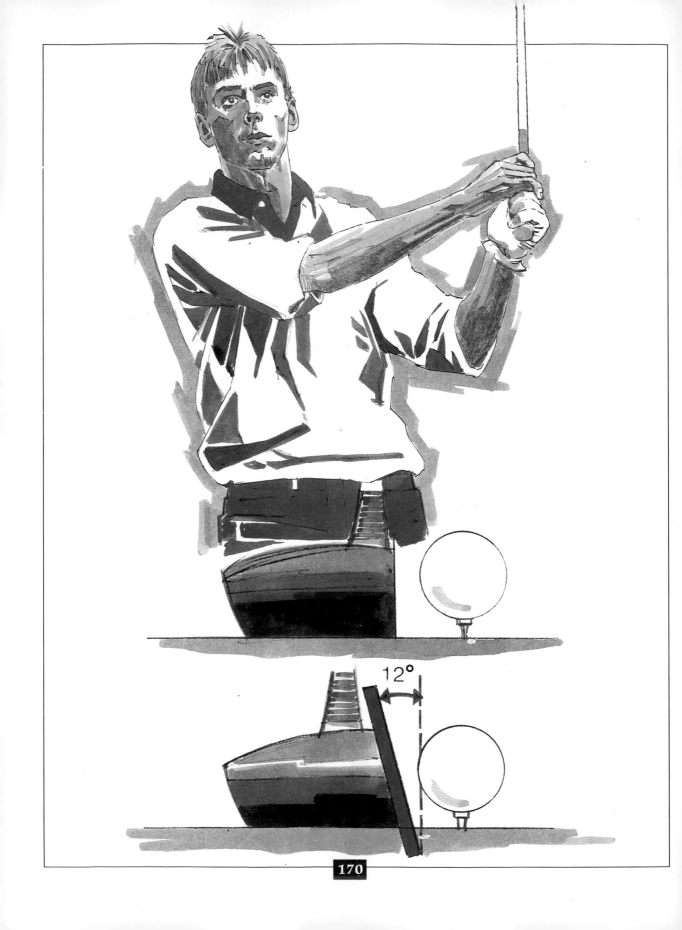

12°

· BRETT OGLE ·

Height: 6ft 2ins. Weight: 10st 8lbs. Birth date: 14 July 1964.
Birthplace: Sydney, Australia

Ogle is one of the thinnest professionals on the European Tour but he still hits the ball a long way thanks to a clubhead speed that has been computer measured at 119 mph. Nicknamed 'Lucky' after a rebounding ball off a tree fractured his knee, Ogle has won all over Asia as well as enjoying success in Europe, where his greatest success to date is lifting the coveted individual title in the 1992 World Cup.

The Tip

MACHO GOLF

To all mid-handicap golfers, I would say 'Don't bother buying a driver'. A two-wood is much easier to hit than a one-wood. I see too many amateur golfers trying to hit a straight-faced driver. Instead I would recommend that you spend a little time looking for a more lofted wood; one with at least 12 degrees of loft if not more. In fact I would like to see a mid-range player exist on a three-wood. All too often I see macho-men grabbing their drivers and trying to belt the living daylights out of the ball. Sure, it might go a long way – sometimes. But where? I would guarantee that if you use a wood with less loft off the tee then you will be on the fairway more often which will lead to you shaving shots off your handicap. And with the right wood in your hands, I honestly don't think you will lose too much in length. So do yourself a favour and go shopping – you know it makes sense.

HEALTHY GOLF

More and more amateur sportsmen are showing an interest in healthy living and golf is a game which demands that all individuals understand how best to take care of themselves. It might be a more gentle sport than football and rugby although Nick Faldo has suffered stress fractures of his wrists causing him to take time out and Richard Boxall broke a leg while driving off during the Open Championship at Royal Birkdale in 1991.

In 1990 the John Hopkins Medical Health Letter, published in the United States, pointed out six things people should do to stay clear of injuries while playing the game. They are all tips which the amateur golfer would do well to heed.

1. Before teeing-off, loosen up by bending slowly from the waist, with your knees bent. Let your arms and head dangle and hold this position for 15 or 20 seconds. Do this several times.

2. Also, before you tee-off, swing your driver from side to side, like a baseball bat, 15 times, gradually extending your swing.

3. Occasionally make a few swings from the opposite direction. That is, if you're right-handed, swing left-handed. This will help keep your body in balance.

4. To help keep your posture upright, as you walk occasionally hold a club across your back in the crook of your elbows.

5. When picking anything up, or teeing your ball, always bend from the knees. Avoid putting strain on your lower back. People have thrown their backs out simply picking a ball out of the cup.

6. When you putt, flex your knees to avoid excessive bending and stress on the lower back.

CHECK IT OUT

· SEVE BALLESTEROS ·

'I don't trust doctors. They are like golfers. Every one has a different answer to your problem.'

(For biographical details, see p.11.)

(For biographical details, see p.11.)

The Tip

WEAK STRENGTH

First work out what is the weakest part of your game and then practise it. A lot of amateurs either don't practise at all or else they only practise the shot they feel comfortable with anyway. Good players, however, will practise their weak link over and over again. The theory is that you work on it until this part of your game becomes one of your strongest suits then you switch to what is THEN your weakest part and work on that. This means, of course, that it is a never ending process, but then that's golf and that's also how you get better at it.

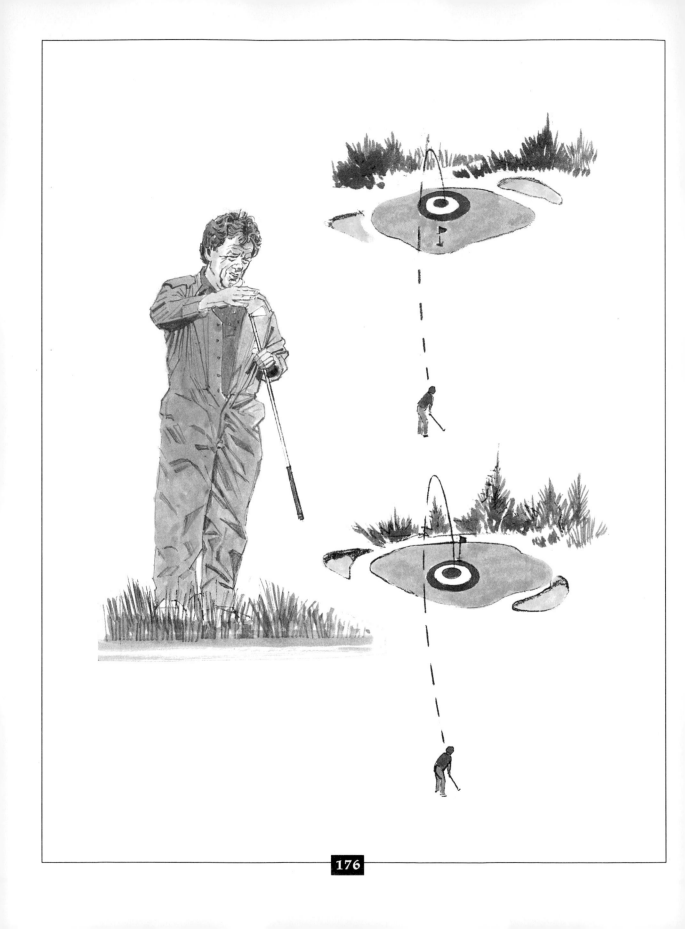

· PETER COLEMAN ·

'People ask me how Bernhard stood up to all that pressure over the last three holes of the Ryder Cup. How about me? I not only had to stand up, I had to carry the bag as well.' Coleman speaking after the 1991 Ryder Cup at Kiawah Island where Langer missed a final six-foot putt to give America victory.

(For biographical details, see p.55.)

(For biographical details, see p.55.)

The Tip

CHOOSING THE RIGHT CLUB

Frequently a golf spectator will see a professional and his caddie in earnest discussion about what club to use for an approach shot to a green. How we sort out this problem can help you too next time you are between, say, a six and a seven iron. First, the general rule: if there are no other factors to take into consideration — bunkers, water in front of the green or behind it for example — I always recommend choosing the shorter iron simply because it is always easier to try to hit the ball a bit harder than it is to take the longer club and try to hit a softer shot. This is hard enough for the best players to do; for most club golfers it ends up a recipe for disaster.

But the important factor, often, if not always, ignored by the amateur, is the position of the hole on the green. Often I ask amateurs whether they would take the six or seven iron if the pin was at the front. They almost always think this means they should take a shorter club. In fact the opposite is true. With the pin at the front, you opt for the longer iron; with the pin at the back, you go with the shorter iron. Why? Because this way, if you hit the ball properly, you should hit the heart of the green and if you do that on every green you will never be far from the flag. With the pin at the front, the shorter club might fetch up short of the putting green leaving you a nasty pitch. Similarly, with the pin at the back, the longer iron might carry everything and find trouble off the back of the green. Simple really, when you think about it.

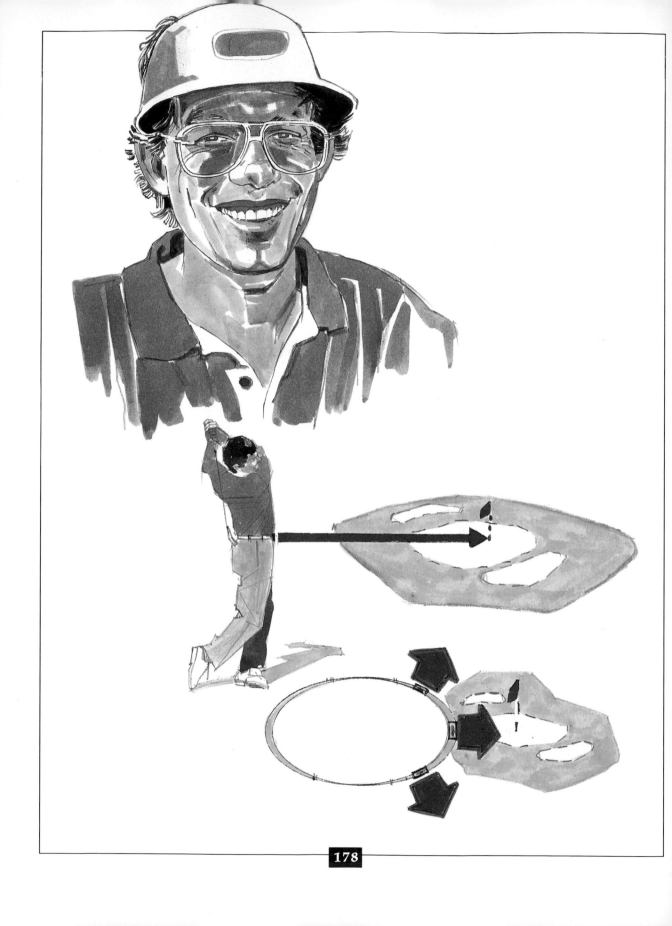

· GAVIN LEVENSON ·

Height: 5ft 7ins. Weight: 10st. Birth date: 18 December 1953.
Birthplace: Johannesburg, South Africa

Levenson has been a regular winner on his native South African Tour throughout the last 10 years but needed less patience before hitting the jackpot in Europe. When he won the 1979 Belgian Open many critics felt he was destined to win several more titles in Europe. But Levenson, chairman of the South African PGA, was compelled to wait until 1991 for his next European success in the Open de Baleares.

The Tip

THE OLD BUCKLE TRICK

One of the old tricks of the trade is to use your belt buckle to see if you are facing the target on the completion of your follow through. To hit straight at the target, then your body must point straight ahead. If the belt buckle is pointing to the left on completion then it is quite likely that you have allowed your swing to become loose and sloppy. If the buckle points to the right then it is likely that you have restricted your hips during the hitting area.

· PAUL AZINGER ·

Height: 6ft 2ins. Weight: 12st. Birth date: 6 January 1960.
Birthplace: Holyoke, Montana, USA

Since the mid-eighties Azinger has been one of the most consistent golfers in America with more than $4 million in prize money to his credit. Tall and slim, he has a deceptively lazy swing action that propels the ball prodigious distances. A devout Christian, he first enjoyed international attention at the 1987 Open Championship at Muirfield, when he led by one stroke with two holes left only to lose to Nick Faldo after problems with a bunker at the last.

The Tip

PAINT THAT LINE

I think a good motto in golf is 'Paint the line of the shot with the clubhead.' You see most amateurs can see the line of a putt, but they fail to extend that thought to the rest of their game. You've got to try to visualise the line of every shot you are going to hit whether it is with the driver, the sand wedge or the putter. In other words if you've got to go into the green from the right then think about how you are going to shape the shot from right to left. And trace the line of the shot by painting that line with the clubhead and then swing the clubhead through that line.

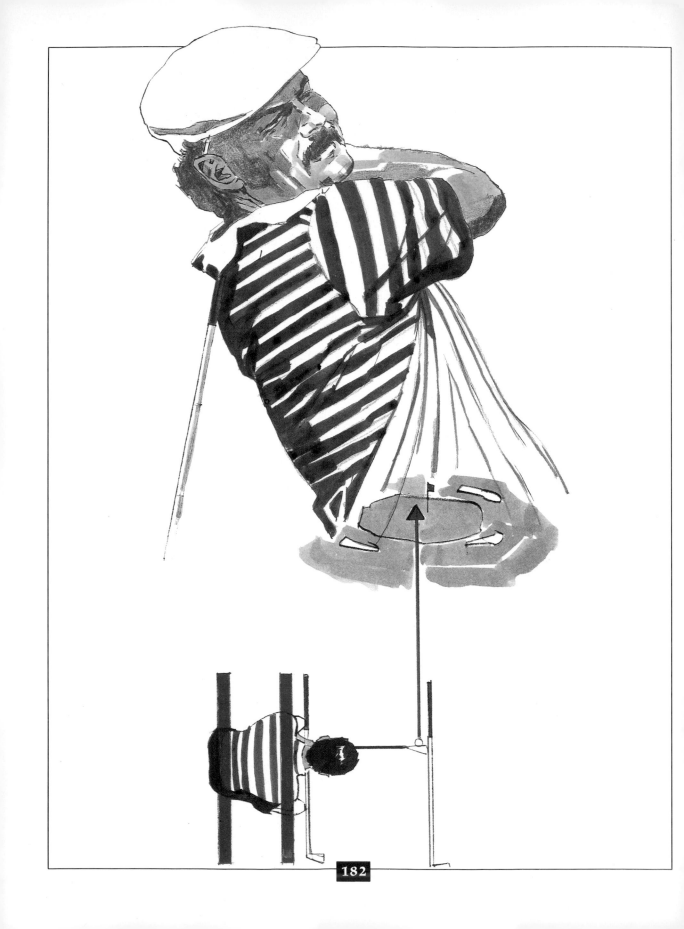

· GORDON BRAND Jnr ·

Height: 5ft 8ins. Weight: 11st 7lbs. Birth date: 19 August 1958.
Birthplace: Kirkcaldy, Scotland

Brand Junior won six top amateur titles, including the British Youths Open, before turning professional in 1982. His success was instant with two Tour titles in his first year which not surprisingly won him the Rookie of the Year title as well. Since then this Scot with a Bristol accent – his family moved south when he was still a child – has lived up to his early promise, winning regularly and adding two Ryder Cup appearances so far to his Walker Cup honour.

The Tip

TWO CLUBS TO REMEMBER

The tip of a lifetime? Take two weeks off... then give up the game completely! No, seriously, the best tip I was ever given was to check my alignment – where you're aiming in terms of your shoulders, hips and hands all being lined up in the right position. I say that without fear of contradiction because more often than not if you stand at a golf club on a Sunday and watch where people are aiming then you will see where most amateurs go wrong from the start. In other words if you don't load the gun properly then you will never be able to pull the trigger. Most amateurs aim to the right, come over the top of the ball and cut it so that it slices to the right. Then they aim more to the right to compensate and, hey presto, they exaggerate the fault. The tip here is not to compensate but to go back to basics. The professionals do... so why not the amateurs? I like to think that the first thing I ever do if something is wrong is to check my swing, check that shoulder alignment and check my posture. I keep to basics because 99 times out of 100 that is where the fault lies. And alignment is so important. The easiest way to check your alignment is to put down two clubs – one to show where you are aiming and the other denoting your ball position. Then get your feet, shoulders and hips aiming down the line on which you want to hit the ball. Most amateurs with whom I've played need to work on their address situation and I believe this simple way of lining-up will help.

· ANDREW CHANDLER ·

Now a successful manager and businessman, Bolton-born Chandler was one of the 'old school' on the European Tour. Although he never quite fulfilled his potential on Tour, he was good enough to become Champion of Brazil and to play in Europe for well over a decade.

MOVE DOWN THE GRIP

If you are between clubs it's a good bet that on most occasions it will be better to take one more than one less. Quite honestly most amateurs come up short of the hole, so if you are longer then you will probably find the putting surface better as fewer golfers will be walking behind the hole. But the key to taking one more club is simple – you can always choke down the grip and take a full swing in the knowledge that you will not hit the ball as far as normal with that club. It also means you can still 'go at the shot' which will reduce the likelihood of you losing your rhythm and so fluffing the shot. It would be a good idea on the practice range when you are swinging well to move your hands down the grip inch by inch to see what difference it makes to the length of shot you hit.

LEAVE THE
BACKSPIN TO
THE PROS

· RUSSELL CLAYDON ·

'People are always commentating about my unusual grip and I've even read that if I don't change to a more orthodox method I won't do well. I take no notice really. I think each of us has to find what is best for ourselves and then stick with it.'

(For biographical details, see p.87.)

(For biographical details, see p.87.)

The Tip

FORGET THE SPIN CYCLE

Most amateurs like to copy the pros, which is only natural, but sometimes it is best to go against that trend. For instance I know it looks great to see guys like Greg Norman and Ian Woosnam spinning the ball back on the greens but in general terms I would recommend that you stick to watching them do that rather than copying them. To begin with it's a tough shot — you've got to hit down on the ball, hit it cleanly — not fat or thin — and the strike must be precise. Norman spins it a lot because he hits a high, cut shot whereas a guy like Steve Richardson, who draws the ball, will never impart so much spin on it. The trick is to live with what you've got and learn instead to judge how far the ball is going to run on. There are very few instances when you need to spin it and if you asked Greg or Ian, I would guess that they would prefer at times if they didn't get so much spin. The ideal shot? The one that stops dead on the second bounce — but that's perfection.

· SIR HENRY COTTON ·

Born in Holmes Chapel, Cheshire in 1907, Sir Henry died in his beloved Portugal in 1987 just a few weeks after learning that he was to be knighted. His three Open victories in 1934, 1937 and 1948 make him one of the finest British golfers of all time but he will also be remembered for the way in which he upgraded the role of the professional golfer at a time when pros were not even allowed into most clubhouses. Sir Henry remained devoted to the game until he died and hardly a day went by without him expounding yet another theory about how golf should be played.

The Tip

FIND THAT BALL

Henry always stressed the importance of being able to 'find the ball'. We were both fortunate to spend several winters in Henry's company at Penina, the golf course he designed and built in the Algarve of Portugal, and Henry would always pass on the most simple of tips to improve our games. He once said that rather than waste the opportunity between shots that you should walk with a club in your hand trying to knock the heads off the tops of daisies, clip the grass or whatever. Henry insisted this was a wonderful way of helping you to 'find the ball'.

· BRUCE CRITCHLEY ·

Born in December 1942, Critchley is one of the last natural amateurs in golf. Good enough to become a Walker Cup player in 1969 and to play for Great Britain versus Europe a year later, he has made his name as a 'sidekick' commentator to Peter Alliss for BBC Television. His laconic and finely drawn words coupled with a natural eye for the game have made him one of the most respected figures in British golf circles.

The Tip

BRAIN DEAD

To improve one's ability to hole out don't let the mind interfere with the quality of the shot. Concentrate on seeing the ball, picturing the ball going into the hole, rather than allowing the brain to think about the quality of the strike. All too often we try much too hard to mechanically put the ball into the hole. It is the principle of throwing a screwed-up piece of paper into a waste-paper basket. You try and do it – you miss. You allow it just to happen, do it and it goes in. The hand–eye co-ordination will work for itself. You try and do it yourself and you make a mess of it. If you started to be mechanical when you were driving a car, thinking well my right foot has got to do this and my left foot has got to do this, then the next thing you know is that you've crashed the car. You've got to do things unencumbered; you musn't start thinking with the putter in your hand that you've got to take it back on the inside. It's got to be a natural movement not a mechanical one.

· EAMONN DARCY ·

Height: 6ft 1ins. Weight: 13st 7lbs. Birth date: 7 August 1952.
Birthplace: Delgany, Ireland

One of the most popular golfers on the European Tour, Darcy can also lay claim to the most individual swing. Asked once what his swing thought was as he prepared to lurch at the ball he replied: 'I just determine to give it a dart.' In reality, however, Darcy's darts have been good enough for him to win no fewer than 12 tournaments, more than £1 million and to play in the 1975, 1977, 1981 and 1987 Ryder Cup matches.

The Tip

WATCH THE BIRDIE

I reckon some good advice is to try to watch the ball a little longer than you normally do. One of the reasons why people, including professionals, hit a lot of bad shots is that there is a slight movement with the head. With the amateur that fault is often exaggerated. But watch any good player when he is playing well and his head stays absolutely still. I remember once when I was not playing well and I couldn't figure out why. Then I played a friendly round with Christy O'Connor Snr and I asked if he would take a look at me. He said that I was swinging the club fine but he told me to just watch the ball a little longer. The trick to that is to keep your head still for as long as you can. Then you can keep watching the back of the ball which will help everything to rotate properly during the swing around your head. It's like an axle.

· NICK FALDO ·

'I think I've always realised that the harder I work in practice, the easier it is to play well in a tournament. When I was a young pro I got a reputation for being stand-offish because I didn't join the other guys in the bar. Well, it was because I was on the range or the putting green trying to improve my technique in some way. You can't have it both ways.'

(For biographical details, see p.95.)

(For biographical details, see p.95.)

The Tip

MIRROR, MIRROR ON THE WALL

If I've learned one thing about golf it is simply this: if you are not in the correct position at address then you can forget trying to make a good score. And this applies to everyone who plays, no matter what their natural ability at hitting the ball. Professionals, amateurs, all of us, should constantly check their address position. You should look for where your feet are, where your shoulders are pointing, whether your hands are in the right position in relation to the ball. I do this all the time. Constantly. I spend time every day in front of the mirror checking my address. If the average club player did the same thing for a couple of minutes every day then he or she would be amazed at how their game improves. All you have to do is to lay a club down so that it points in the chosen position and then line up to it, relating hips and knees and shoulders to feet. It's simple. And it's essential.

PAR 5 DOG LEG

· DAVE STOCKTON ·

Height: 5ft 11½ins. Weight: 13st. Birth date: 2 November 1941.
Birthplace: San Bernadino, California, USA

Stockton first played on the US Tour in 1964 and swiftly established a reputation as one of the finest short-game players in the USA. Since then he has won 11 Tour titles, including the US PGA Championships in 1970 and 1976. Now on the Seniors Tour in America, Stockton captained the 1991 US Ryder Cup team to victory at Kiawah Island.

The Tip

A THINKING MAN'S GAME

All of us should use our brains more on the golf course. I remember once speaking to a bunch of American club pros and when I asked how many of them had ever given a club member a lesson by simply sitting down and talking to him or her about how to play the game, only about five guys put up their hands. That's awful. Too often too many of us concentrate on the physical side of the game and neglect the mental. Yet if we could only think our way round all the time then all our games would benefit. If you have a handicap then use it. There's no point going for that once a year four iron to a difficult green if a five iron will leave you within easy pitching distance and you have a shot on the hole. There's no point either, automatically reaching for your driver on every tee. Look at each hole, plot your way through every hole, think about what you are doing, what *you* are capable of and your game will improve immediately.

· WAYNE GRADY ·

Height: 5ft 9ins. Weight: 12st. Birth date: 26 July 1957.
Birthplace: Brisbane, Australia

Grady's distinctive limp – one leg is shorter than the other – is now a familiar and welcome sight on the world's fairways. For much of his career this modest golfer has played in the shadow of his extrovert countryman Greg Norman but victory in the 1990 US PGA and a play-off for the Open, which he lost to Mark Calcavecchia in 1989, have established his own credentials and his right to be mentioned in the same breath as the world's best golfers.

The Tip

BE AWARE OF THE BALL

One tip to improve someone's game? That's easy...*Watch* the ball. By this I don't mean stare the paint off the ball but, please, do concentrate on seeing the ball throughout the swing. Almost invariably any time any of us do not see the ball as we swing back and through, we hit a bad shot. Most golfers get fired up about where the ball is going and automatically their heads lift as they swing through. It is a natural reaction to the thought. Start wondering where the ball is going and you can forget about it because you will top it. So, from tomorrow, 'Be aware of the ball' at all times.

· BARRY LANE ·

Height: 5ft 10ins. Weight: 12st 7lbs. Birth date: 21 June 1960.
Birthplace: Hayes, England

Recognised by contemporaries as one of the strongest players on the European Tour, Lane won the 1988 Bell's Scottish Open. His three stroke triumph at Gleneagles underlined what has always been a natural talent, confirmed when he added the German Masters in 1992. A Dunhill Cup and World Cup player, Lane signalled his ability by winning the British and World Assistants Championship plus the Jamaica Open in 1983.

The Tip

CHECK THOSE FEET

If you start hitting too many off-target shots then one reason could be that the ball is positioned incorrectly at address. When driving, the ball should be positioned in line with the left heel. Often enough you will think you are doing that when in fact you are not. The best way to make sure you have got it right is to place a club down on the ground pointing out from your left heel at right angles to another club to which you take your stance. You might be surprised to discover that you actually have the ball several inches too far back, or too far forward for that matter, at address.

· SANDY LYLE ·

'When I started having problems with my game I got hundreds of letters offering me various remedies. One guy even sent me videos of war films to remind me how great it is to be British.'

(For biographical details, see p.39.)

The Tip

HANDS TOGETHER

Most amateurs get very strong with the left hand. They start showing three or four knuckles. Then they can't get the right hand to sit comfortably on top of the left. So the left hand naturally takes charge, and from then it's all a bit of a disaster. The clubface will tend to close on the backswing and remain that way through impact, which will certainly lead to a hook.

The way to take a correct grip is to put the club down square behind the ball and then keep both palms of the hand facing each other. You should now be able to see one to one-and-half knuckles on the back of the left hand. The club should be gripped so that it runs from the base of the little finger to the middle of the forefinger.

· NICK FALDO ·

'I've had to accept that I simply cannot please all of the people all of the time. I once said that I loved Scotland, the people, the countryside, even the porridge. Shortly afterwards a Scottish reporter asked me why I didn't like Scotland...'

(For biographical details, see p.95.)

The Tip

FIX THOSE KNEES

The big thing is to keep your legs solid. If your legs are flying around, especially your knees, then you've got no hope of keeping your head still. You must have a solid base; that is the start to a solid swing. And you don't need to go onto a big weight-training programme to get the base you need. You just need to learn to keep your legs fixed. The key to that is to learn to put some pressure on them...a little resistance.

· JACK NICKLAUS ·

'After I won my sixth US Masters in 1986 I did think for a little bit that I could still do it. But I wasn't quite there with the things I needed. That's when I started realising – I'm fooling myself if I think I'm as good as I was 15 years ago.'

(For biographical details, see p.17.)

(For biographical details, see p.17.)

The Tip

MARK THE TARGET LINE

Is it easier to hit a target three feet away or one some 250 yards distant? The answer is obvious. So it must stand to reason that it is easier to line yourself up at the target by looking at an object directly in line but only three feet away. It is a routine I thought up years ago and I have used it ever since whether on the tee, the fairway or in the rough. I use a blade of grass, a small stone, a weed, anything to line myself up properly because if I'm not aiming correctly at the target I have no chance of hitting it no matter how well I actually strike the ball. Yet most amateurs carry on trying to line up with a target too far away to see clearly. I've lost count of the number of times I've seen amateurs, some of them decent players as well, aiming miles off-target because of this tendency to look at the green, the flag, or whatever, and then look straight down at their ball.

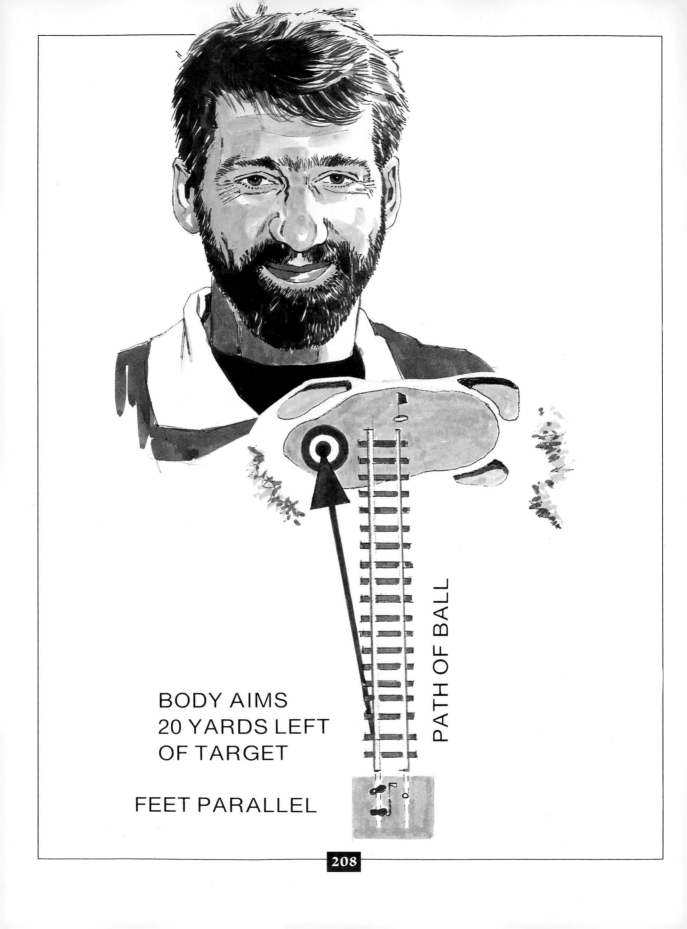

BODY AIMS
20 YARDS LEFT
OF TARGET

FEET PARALLEL

PATH OF BALL

· FRANK NOBILO ·

Height: 5ft 11ins. Weight: 13st. Birth date: 14 May 1960.
Birthplace: Auckland, New Zealand

The bearded Kiwi is the best to emerge from New Zealand since Bob Charles made being left-handed fashionable. Nobilo is a proven winner both in Europe and elsewhere and is known for his ability to score well when his game is temporarily off. Apart from golf, his proudest claim is to be a direct descendant of a Mediterranean pirate.

The Tip

THE RAILWAY LINE

If there is one thing that all amateurs must look at it is their set-up. Out of the people I've played with in Pro-Ams, 90 per cent aim to the right. That is the main reason why 90 per cent of amateurs slice the ball because it makes them come across their body. In contrast you will find most professionals suffer from a hook. That is because the set-up they use develops more power, more turn, more body action, whereas most amateurs, because of their set-up, use their arms too much. I think the best way to go about improving the set-up is to put a club down on the practice fairway, pointing in the intended direction. Then make sure that the body is fairly evenly parallel and that the shoulders, hips, knees and feet are all pointing roughly 20 yards left of the target. It is the old railway line theory. You see, the eyes are the biggest tricksters. When you look at the target, instinctively you look straight at the hole but your body has to be parallel to that and not actually aiming at it. Therefore the swing will be more of a circular action, whereas most players hit very much up and down the line and that actually results in hitting across the ball.

209

ALLOW FOR THE SLICE

· STEVE PATE ·

Height: 6ft. Weight: 12st. Birth date: 26 May 1961.
Birthplace: Ventura, California, USA

Pate hit the headlines for all the wrong reasons in 1991 when he was injured in a car crash on his way to a Ryder Cup Ball in Charleston. But if this was a low point, Pate's recent years have been filled with success on the US Tour. This quiet American began playing golf at nine years of age and shot 107 during his first serious competition as an 11-year-old.

The Tip

GO WITH THE FLOW

Everyone knows that individual form in golf is unpredictable. It is one of the ingredients of the game that makes it so fascinating and, at times, so frustrating. One day you go out at your local club and feel just right, rhythm and timing spot on. The next day, hopes raised, you stride to the first tee and everything goes wrong. Well, it's pretty much the same even for the top professionals. Where we differ is in our ability to *score* reasonably on these off-days. And one of the ways we do that is because we do not fight the swing we bring to the tee. For example, I often suffer from a vicious slice. When that happens I *play* with it. I don't try to adjust anything out there on the course because that can lead to disaster and I can end up so much out of line that I really suffer. Instead I allow for my slice. If I'm standing on the tee and there's trouble on the right then I aim way over to the left. Do the same whatever your problem is on any particular day. If your timing is off and you simply are not hitting the ball as well as usual then allow for that by moving down a club. Hitting your five iron fat? Then use a four iron for what would normally be your five iron distance and so on. And then as soon as the round is over go spend half an hour on the practice range ironing out your fault. That's the place to experiment and correct, *not* the course. That's where you play – and go with what you've got for that day!

· SAM TORRANCE ·

Height: 5ft 11ins. Weight: 13st 7lbs. Birth date: 24 August 1953.
Birthplace: Largs, Scotland

Torrance will be remembered forever as the man who sank the winning birdie putt at The Belfry in 1985 when Europe beat America in the Ryder Cup for the first time since 1957. But there is much more to this highly respected and likeable Scot than this one putt. Born the son of a pro, his appetite for the game was prodigious from the start and six consecutive Ryder Cup appearances from 1981 highlights his continuing enthusiasm for a game that has made him rich as well as famous. He has won fifteen European titles so far in a pro career that began back in 1970 when he was just 17.

The Tip

LOOSEN UP AT THE START

I think a good tip is to hold the club much lighter at address. The reason? Because automatically when you take the club back, you tighten-up. So if you're gripping it tight at address, you are going to be too tight at the top and you will lose feel and control. It should be as if you are holding two eggs at address. If you are too tight you will have no feel there. Don't think that you are going to let go of the club because the grip will automatically tighten on the way back.

· MARK McNULTY ·

Height: 5ft 10ins. Weight: 11st 4lbs. Birth date: 25 October 1953.
Birthplace: Zimbabwe

Recognised as one of the most consistent golfers ever to play the European Tour, McNulty's lowest end-of-year position in Europe since 1986 has been 11th. In 1990 he played 14 consecutive events and never once ended outside the top four. Eleven European titles so far plus double that number won abroad underline his talent for the game in general and his ability to seize victory when the chance presents itself in particular. He turned professional in 1977 and has won the South African Order of Merit four times.

The Tip

COMPETE WITH YOURSELF

Let us get one thing straight from the start. If you have a handicap of, say, 14 you must learn to use it — not fight it. I believe most amateurs stand on the first tee without fully understanding why they have a handicap. It is there to use to your advantage. The best way to do that is not to try to play like the five-handicapper you are not. Don't try to emulate your partner if he plays off a lower handicap than you. It must seem logical that if you were playing against me with a handicap of 14, then it would be absolutely foolish to take me on shot for shot. The moment you start to do that then you are beaten. You won't even play near to your own handicap. It's no different for me if I get onto a tennis court with Boris Becker. I know I couldn't even come close to emulating his style of play. But I've seen many amateur golfers stand on the first tee with a professional and over-swing trying to hit the ball the proverbial country mile. Where does it go — into the woods! The next moment he's looking at this little gap through the branches. He's seen Seve Ballesteros thread a similar shot onto the green in a recent tournament on TV and he reckons he can do it. Now the ball hits a tree and ricochets out of bounds. In other words he's using a number of his shots at one hole. All you've got to do is to play safe from the trees then try to get your next shot on the green. If you do that then you might single putt for your par. Just appreciate that you can't play all the shots that a professional hits but that if you take your handicap into account at all times then you will be able to beat lower handicap opponents simply because you're being smart.

· TOMMY HORTON ·

Height: 5ft 8ins. Weight: 9st 7lbs. Birth date: 16 June 1941.
Birthplace: St Helens, Lancashire, England

Horton started life as a pro as a member of the Butten Boys – a group of golfers backed by time-and-motion consultant Ernest Butten – alongside Brian Barnes. He became recognised as one of the best iron players in the game and he won titles such as the PGA Match Play Championship (1970), South African Open (1970), Piccadilly Medal (1972) and Dunlop Masters (1978). He played in the 1975 and 1977 Ryder Cups.

The Tip

A SQUARE DEAL

This is a good exercise which helps you to square the clubface up to the ball which is essential. Set up to the golf ball and with the ball in the correct position for a four iron, or a fairwood wood, take a proper backswing but practise the downswing only. Just check to see that when the club arrives at the golf ball it is square – not open or closed. In other words what has got to happen is the hands and the golf clubhead have got to be level at the impact position. All slicers will find that their hands are ahead and all hookers that their hands are behind. But if their hands and the clubhead are level at the impact position then you will know you are squaring the clubface to the ball. You'll be set for the round of your life.

· PETER ALLISS ·

Born in Berlin on 28 February 1931, Alliss followed in his father's footsteps and became a professional golfer in 1946. Through the fifties and sixties he became one of the dominant British players with eight Ryder Cup appearances and a shoal of titles. Now generally acknowledged as one of the best commentators on the game in the world, he has twice been captain of the PGA and is the author of numerous books. He now lives in Hindhead, Surrey.

The Tip

THE MAD AXEMAN SYNDROME

The one thing most golfers forget is that you hit the ball with the clubhead and *not* with your belly-button. Let me explain what I mean. If you are walking through the woods with a walking stick, it is easy to swing at a fir cone. Nobody misses the fir cone in this situation. yet so many golfers turn into a sort of mad axeman the moment they pick up a club and try to hit the ball. They immediately switch to using brute strength and try to literally club the ball to death. Instead, try to stand balanced and reasonably relaxed, hold the club with your hands and try to 'feel' that clubhead. Feel it and remember that this is what will hit the ball and that it is an extension of your body, not an axehead. Try to feel the ball come off the clubhead, be it metal or wood, and I promise you that your whole golfing life will become simpler and better.

5 IRON
TO
4 IRON

· FUZZY ZOELLER ·

Height: 5ft 10ins. Weight: 13st 5lbs. Birth date: 11 November 1951.
Birthplace: New Albany, Indiana, USA

Nicknamed Fuzzy because of his initials, Francis Urban Zoeller is a winner of the US Open and US Masters. A natural extrovert, Zoeller delights in entertaining crowds and is a favourite of the galleries all over the world. Although impressive, his career record of 10 US Tour victories would have been even better were it not for the severe back trouble which has restricted his playing schedule since the mid-eighties.

The Tip

MOVE UP TO MOVE ON

Every time I play with an amateur I see the same problem again and again — they all play one club short. My advice is simple: work out the distance you wish to hit the ball, work out which club you feel you would use to hit the ball that far and then move up a club. If you think you need to hit a five iron to the green then hit a four instead and so on. How many times do amateurs go through the green with a decently hit shot? Hardly ever, in my experience. They all think that they are going to hit their best possible shot but the truth is that they rarely do and so often they are well short of the target. So change the club *up* — and change your luck.

· JOSE MARIA OLAZABAL ·

Height: 5ft 10ins. Weight: 11st. Birth date: 5 February 1966.
Birthplace: Fuenterrabia, Spain

Olazabal is a phenomenon. As an amateur he won the British, Spanish, Italian and Belgian titles before turning professional in 1985 just after the Open Championship. By the end of 1986 he had won twice in Europe and finished the year as runner-up in the official Money List. Since then he has finished 17th, 3rd, 2nd, 3rd and 2nd and has earned more than £2 million already in Europe alone. Victories in America and Japan and a runner-up in the 1991 US Masters merely whet the appetite for what is surely to come from the most outrageously talented golfer of his generation.

The Tip

BECOME A FILM STAR

I think it is all important that any amateur, no matter to what standard he or she plays, understands their own swing. It is only through knowing how you swing the club that you can hope to improve. Initially it is imperative that you have a good understanding of the basics. But then you must take time to study your own swing because every swing is different somewhere. The importance of this is that if you start to play badly, and that happens to all of us, you can in this modern day take a look at your swing on video. You can compare the swing to how it looks when you are playing well. Therefore you should have a video of your swing when all is O.K. You must look at that time and time again to see how you are swinging the club when you are playing to the best of your ability. The key lesson to be learned from this is that you must at all times know in your mind what you are aiming to achieve. It is pointless to go to the practice range with no idea of what you need to do to correct your swing. But if you know your swing well, then you will be able to find what is wrong. Then you can cure it and improve your game.